Spanish Verb Conjugation Quick Reference

Drizzle
Books

Published by Drizzle Books in 2012
Copyright © Drizzle Books 2012

Publishing director: Baoyan Wu
Contributors: Carla Davis, Miriam Sanchez
Cover design: Baoyan Wu

ISBN: 978-0-9574115-0-0

CONTENTS

Introduction

Spanish Verb Conjugation Quick Reference is designed to
help you get to grips with Spanish verb conjugation which
can be quite a challenge for students of Spanish. This
handy book aims to provide you with quick help whether
you want to refresh your memory of a certain verb form or
wish to study Spanish verbs thoroughly.

This book is mainly made up of two parts: verb tables and
a verb index. The verb tables, all numbered to facilitate
cross-reference, illustrate the conjugation of 95 model
verbs. The first three tables cover regular verbs ending in -
ar, -er and -ir respectively; tables numbered 4–95 deal with
irregular verbs arranged in alphabetical order. In a table,
irregular forms are highlighted to help the user quickly
identify the specificities of the verb. At the bottom of each
table, other verbs that follow the same pattern are
included. Some verbs, such as *estar*, are unique in their
conjugation and no other verbs share the same pattern.

The verb index contains more than 4000 commonly used
verbs. The number following each verb indicates which
model verb table you should refer to for the conjugation
pattern. For instance, if you want to know about
abandonar, the number "(1)" next to it indicates that
abandonar follows the pattern of regular model verb *amar*
whose table number is "1". If you want to find out about
conseguir, the number "(82)" next to it cross-refers you to
verb table No. 82 where *seguir* is conjugated. In the index,
verbs marked in bold are model verbs. Please note that the
numbers next to the verbs refer to verb table numbers, not
page numbers.

At the end of this book, also for your quick reference, an appendix of formation of Spanish verb tenses and moods is included, covering simple and compound tenses, reflexive and non-reflexive verbs.

We hope that *Spanish Verb Conjugation Quick Reference* will serve as an effective reference tool for students and teachers of Spanish.

Verb Tables

1. amar (to love)

PRESENT	PRESENT SUBJUNCTIVE
amo	ame
amas	ames
ama	ame
amamos	amemos
amáis	améis
aman	amen

IMPERFECT	IMPERFECT SUBJUNCTIVE
amaba	amara/amase
amabas	amaras/amases
amaba	amara/amase
amábamos	amáramos/amásemos
amabais	amarais/amaseis
amaban	amaran/amasen

FUTURE	CONDITIONAL
amaré	amaría
amarás	amarías
amará	amaría
amaremos	amaríamos
amaréis	amaríais
amarán	amarían

PRETERITE	IMPERATIVE
amé	ama, amad
amaste	
amó	GERUND
amamos	amando
amasteis	
amaron	PAST PARTICIPLE
	amado

2. comer (to eat)

PRESENT
como
comes
come
comemos
coméis
comen

PRESENT SUBJUNCTIVE
coma
comas
coma
comamos
comáis
coman

IMPERFECT
comía
comías
comía
comíamos
comíais
comían

IMPERFECT SUBJUNCTIVE
comiera/comiese
comieras/comieses
comiera/comiese
comiéramos/comiésemos
comierais/comieseis
comieran/comiesen

FUTURE
comeré
comerás
comerá
comeremos
comeréis
comerán

CONDITIONAL
comería
comerías
comería
comeríamos
comeríais
comerían

PRETERITE
comí
comiste
comió
comimos
comisteis
comieron

IMPERATIVE
come, comed

GERUND
comiendo

PAST PARTICIPLE
comido

3. vivir (to live)

PRESENT	PRESENT SUBJUNCTIVE
vivo	viva
vives	vivas
vive	viva
vivimos	vivamos
vivís	viváis
viven	vivan

IMPERFECT	IMPERFECT SUBJUNCTIVE
vivía	viviera/viviese
vivías	vivieras/vivieses
vivía	viviera/viviese
vivíamos	viviéramos/viviésemos
vivíais	vivierais/vivieseis
vivían	vivieran/viviesen

FUTURE	CONDITIONAL
viviré	viviría
vivirás	vivirías
vivirá	viviría
viviremos	viviríamos
viviréis	viviríais
vivirán	vivirían

PRETERITE	IMPERATIVE
viví	vive, vivid
viviste	
vivió	GERUND
vivimos	viviendo
vivisteis	
vivieron	PAST PARTICIPLE
	vivido

4. abolir (to abolish)

PRESENT	PRESENT SUBJUNCTIVE
-	-
-	-
-	-
abolimos	-
abolís	-
-	-

IMPERFECT	IMPERFECT SUBJUNCTIVE
abolía	aboliera/aboliese
abolías	abolieras/abolieses
abolía	aboliera/aboliese
abolíamos	aboliéramos/aboliésemos
abolíais	abolierais/abolieseis
abolían	abolieran/aboliesen

FUTURE	CONDITIONAL
aboliré	aboliría
abolirás	abolirías
abolirá	aboliría
aboliremos	aboliríamos
aboliréis	aboliríais
abolirán	abolirían

PRETERITE	IMPERATIVE
abolí	-, abolid
aboliste	
abolió	GERUND
abolimos	aboliendo
abolisteis	
abolieron	PAST PARTICIPLE
	abolido

Other verbs that follow this model:
agredir, aguerrir, arrecirse, aterirse, balbucir, blandir,
empedernir, garantir, manir, transgredir, trasgredir

5. abrir (to open)

PRESENT	PRESENT SUBJUNCTIVE
abro	abra
abres	abras
abre	abra
abrimos	abramos
abrís	abráis
abren	abran

IMPERFECT	IMPERFECT SUBJUNCTIVE
abría	abriera/abriese
abrías	abrieras/abrieses
abría	abriera/abriese
abríamos	abriéramos/abriésemos
abríais	abrierais/abrieseis
abrían	abrieran/abriesen

FUTURE	CONDITIONAL
abriré	abriría
abrirás	abrirías
abrirá	abriría
abriremos	abriríamos
abriréis	abriríais
abrirán	abrirían

PRETERITE	IMPERATIVE
abrí	abre, abrid
abriste	
abrió	GERUND
abrimos	abriendo
abristeis	
abrieron	PAST PARTICIPLE
	abierto

Other verbs that follow this model:
cubrir, descubrir, encubrir, entreabrir, reabrir, recubrir, redescubrir

6. actuar (to act)

PRESENT	PRESENT SUBJUNCTIVE
actúo	**actú**e
actúas	**actú**es
actúa	**actú**e
actuamos	actuemos
actuáis	actuéis
actúan	**actú**en

IMPERFECT	IMPERFECT SUBJUNCTIVE
actuaba	actuara/actuase
actuabas	actuaras/actuases
actuaba	actuara/actuase
actuábamos	actuáramos/actuásemos
actuabais	actuarais/actuaseis
actuaban	actuaran/actuasen

FUTURE	CONDITIONAL
actuaré	actuaría
actuarás	actuarías
actuará	actuaría
actuaremos	actuaríamos
actuaréis	actuaríais
actuarán	actuarían

PRETERITE	IMPERATIVE
actué	**actú**a, actuad
actuaste	
actuó	GERUND
actuamos	actuando
actuasteis	
actuaron	PAST PARTICIPLE
	actuado

Other verbs that follow this model:
acentuar, atenuar, conceptuar, consensuar, continuar, desconceptuar, deshabituar, desvirtuar, devaluar, efectuar,

Verb Tables

evaluar, exceptuar, extenuar, fluctuar, garuar, graduar, habituar, insinuar, interactuar, licuar, perpetuar, puntuar, redituar, revaluar, situar, tatuar, valuar

7. adquirir (to acquire)

PRESENT	PRESENT SUBJUNCTIVE
adquiero	**adquier**a
adquieres	**adquier**as
adquiere	**adquier**a
adquirimos	adquiramos
adquirís	adquiráis
adquieren	**adquier**an

IMPERFECT	IMPERFECT SUBJUNCTIVE
adquiría	adquiriera/adquiriese
adquirías	adquirieras/adquirieses
adquiría	adquiriera/adquiriese
adquiríamos	adquiriéramos/adquiriésemos
adquiríais	adquirierais/adquirieseis
adquirían	adquirieran/adquiriesen

FUTURE	CONDITIONAL
adquiriré	adquiriría
adquirirás	adquirirías
adquirirá	adquiriría
adquiriremos	adquiriríamos
adquiriréis	adquiriríais
adquirirán	adquirirían

PRETERITE	IMPERATIVE
adquirí	**adquier**e, adquirid
adquiriste	
adquirió	GERUND
adquirimos	adquiriendo
adquiristeis	
adquirieron	PAST PARTICIPLE
	adquirido

Other verbs that follow this model:
inquirir, readquirir

8. ahincar (to urge)

PRESENT	PRESENT SUBJUNCTIVE
ahínco	**ahínqu**e
ahíncas	**ahínqu**es
ahínca	**ahínqu**e
ahincamos	**ahinqu**emos
ahincáis	**ahinqu**éis
ahíncan	**ahínqu**en

IMPERFECT	IMPERFECT SUBJUNCTIVE
ahincaba	ahincara/ahincase
ahincabas	ahincaras/ahincases
ahincaba	ahincara/ahincase
ahincábamos	ahincáramos/ahincásemos
ahincabais	ahincarais/ahincaseis
ahincaban	ahincaran/ahincasen

FUTURE	CONDITIONAL
ahincaré	ahincaría
ahincarás	ahincarías
ahincará	ahincaría
ahincaremos	ahincaríamos
ahincaréis	ahincaríais
ahincarán	ahincarían

PRETERITE	IMPERATIVE
ahinqué	**ahínc**a, ahincad
ahincaste	
ahincó	GERUND
ahincamos	ahincando
ahincasteis	
ahincaron	PAST PARTICIPLE
	ahincado

10

9. aislar (to isolate)

PRESENT	PRESENT SUBJUNCTIVE
aíslo	**aísl**e
aíslas	**aísl**es
aísla	**aísl**e
aislamos	aislemos
aisláis	aisléis
aíslan	**aísl**en

IMPERFECT	IMPERFECT SUBJUNCTIVE
aislaba	aislara/aislase
aislabas	aislaras/aislases
aislaba	aislara/aislase
aislábamos	aisláramos/aislásemos
aislabais	aislarais/aislaseis
aislaban	aislaran/aislasen

FUTURE	CONDITIONAL
aislaré	aislaría
aislarás	aislarías
aislará	aislaría
aislaremos	aislaríamos
aislaréis	aislaríais
aislarán	aislarían

PRETERITE	IMPERATIVE
aislé	**aísl**a, aislad
aislaste	
aisló	GERUND
aislamos	aislando
aislasteis	
aislaron	PAST PARTICIPLE
	aislado

Other verbs that follow this model:
ahijar, ahilar, ahitar, airar, amohinar, atraillar, desahijar, descafeinar, prohijar, rehilar, sobrehilar

10. almorzar (to have lunch)

PRESENT	PRESENT SUBJUNCTIVE
almuerzo	**almuerc**e
almuerzas	**almuerc**es
almuerza	**almuerc**e
almorzamos	**almorc**emos
almorzáis	**almorc**éis
almuerzan	**almuerc**en

IMPERFECT	IMPERFECT SUBJUNCTIVE
almorzaba	almorzara/almorzase
almorzabas	almorzaras/almorzases
almorzaba	almorzara/almorzase
almorzábamos	almorzáramos/almorzásemos
almorzabais	almorzarais/almorzaseis
almorzaban	almorzaran/almorzasen

FUTURE	CONDITIONAL
almorzaré	almorzaría
almorzarás	almorzarías
almorzará	almorzaría
almorzaremos	almorzaríamos
almorzaréis	almorzaríais
almorzarán	almorzarían

PRETERITE	IMPERATIVE
almorcé	**almuerz**a, almorzad
almorzaste	
almorzó	GERUND
almorzamos	almorzando
almorzasteis	
almorzaron	PAST PARTICIPLE
	almorzado

Other verbs that follow this model:
esforzar, forzar, reforzar

11. andar (to walk)

PRESENT	PRESENT SUBJUNCTIVE
ando	ande
andas	andes
anda	ande
andamos	andemos
andáis	andéis
andan	anden

IMPERFECT	IMPERFECT SUBJUNCTIVE
andaba	anduviera/anduviese
andabas	anduvieras/anduvieses
andaba	anduviera/anduviese
andábamos	anduviéramos/anduviésemos
andabais	anduvierais/anduvieseis
andaban	anduvieran/anduviesen

FUTURE	CONDITIONAL
andaré	andaría
andarás	andarías
andará	andaría
andaremos	andaríamos
andaréis	andaríais
andarán	andarían

PRETERITE	IMPERATIVE
anduve	anda, andad
anduviste	
anduvo	GERUND
anduvimos	andando
anduvisteis	
anduvieron	PAST PARTICIPLE
	andado

Other verbs that follow this model:
desandar

12. argüir (to argue)

PRESENT	PRESENT SUBJUNCTIVE
arguyo	**arguy**a
arguyes	**arguy**as
arguye	**arguy**a
argüimos	**arguy**amos
argüís	**arguy**áis
arguyen	**arguy**an

IMPERFECT	IMPERFECT SUBJUNCTIVE
argüía	**arguyera/arguyese**
argüías	**arguyeras/arguyeses**
argüía	**arguyera/arguyese**
argüíamos	**arguyéramos/arguyésemos**
argüíais	**arguyerais/arguyeseis**
argüían	**arguyeran/arguyesen**

FUTURE	CONDITIONAL
argüiré	argüiría
argüirás	argüirías
argüirá	argüiría
argüiremos	argüiríamos
argüiréis	argüiríais
argüirán	argüirían

PRETERITE	IMPERATIVE
argüí	**arguy**e, argüid
argüiste	
arguyó	GERUND
argüimos	**arguyendo**
argüisteis	
arguyeron	PAST PARTICIPLE
	argüido

Other verbs that follow this model:
reargüir, redargüir

14

13. asir (to seize)

PRESENT	PRESENT SUBJUNCTIVE
asgo	**asg**a
ases	**asg**as
ase	**asg**a
asimos	**asg**amos
asís	**asg**áis
asen	**asg**an

IMPERFECT	IMPERFECT SUBJUNCTIVE
asía	asiera/asiese
asías	asieras/asieses
asía	asiera/asiese
asíamos	asiéramos/asiésemos
asíais	asierais/asieseis
asían	asieran/asiesen

FUTURE	CONDITIONAL
asiré	asiría
asirás	asirías
asirá	asiría
asiremos	asiríamos
asiréis	asiríais
asirán	asirían

PRETERITE	IMPERATIVE
así	ase, asid
asiste	
asió	GERUND
asimos	asiendo
asisteis	
asieron	PAST PARTICIPLE
	asido

Other verbs that follow this model:
desasir

14. aunar (to combine)

PRESENT	PRESENT SUBJUNCTIVE
aúno	**aún**e
aúnas	**aún**es
aúna	**aún**e
aunamos	aunemos
aunáis	aunéis
aúnan	**aún**en

IMPERFECT	IMPERFECT SUBJUNCTIVE
aunaba	aunara/aunase
aunabas	aunaras/aunases
aunaba	aunara/aunase
aunábamos	aunáramos/aunásemos
aunabais	aunarais/aunaseis
aunaban	aunaran/aunasen

FUTURE	CONDITIONAL
aunaré	aunaría
aunarás	aunarías
aunará	aunaría
aunaremos	aunaríamos
aunaréis	aunaríais
aunarán	aunarían

PRETERITE	IMPERATIVE
auné	**aún**a, aunad
aunaste	
aunó	GERUND
aunamos	aunando
aunasteis	
aunaron	PAST PARTICIPLE
	aunado

Other verbs that follow this model:
ahumar, ahusar, aullar, aupar, embaular, maullar, rehusar, sahumar

15. avergonzar (to embarrass)

PRESENT
avergüenzo
avergüenzas
avergüenza
avergonzamos
avergonzáis
avergüenzan

PRESENT SUBJUNCTIVE
avergüence
avergüences
avergüence
avergoncemos
avergoncéis
avergüencen

IMPERFECT
avergonzaba
avergonzabas
avergonzaba
avergonzábamos
avergonzabais
avergonzaban

IMPERFECT SUBJUNCTIVE
avergonzara/avergonzase
avergonzaras/avergonzases
avergonzara/avergonzase
avergonzáramos/avergonzásemos
avergonzarais/avergonzaseis
avergonzaran/avergonzasen

FUTURE
avergonzaré
avergonzarás
avergonzará
avergonzaremos
avergonzaréis
avergonzarán

CONDITIONAL
avergonzaría
avergonzarías
avergonzaría
avergonzaríamos
avergonzaríais
avergonzarían

PRETERITE
avergoncé
avergonzaste
avergonzó
avergonzamos
avergonzasteis
avergonzaron

IMPERATIVE
avergüenza, avergonzad

GERUND
avergonzando

PAST PARTICIPLE
avergonzado

Other verbs that follow this model:
desvergonzarse

16. averiguar (to find out)

PRESENT	PRESENT SUBJUNCTIVE
averiguo	**averigüe**
averiguas	**averigües**
averigua	**averigüe**
averiguamos	**averigüemos**
averiguáis	**averigüéis**
averiguan	**averigüen**

IMPERFECT	IMPERFECT SUBJUNCTIVE
averiguaba	averiguara/averiguase
averiguabas	averiguaras/averiguases
averiguaba	averiguara/averiguase
averiguábamos	averiguáramos/averiguásemos
averiguabais	averiguarais/averiguaseis
averiguaban	averiguaran/averiguasen

FUTURE	CONDITIONAL
averiguaré	averiguaría
averiguarás	averiguarías
averiguará	averiguaría
averiguaremos	averiguaríamos
averiguaréis	averiguaríais
averiguarán	averiguarían

PRETERITE	IMPERATIVE
averigüé	averigua, averiguad
averiguaste	
averiguó	GERUND
averiguamos	averiguando
averiguasteis	
averiguaron	PAST PARTICIPLE
	averiguado

Other verbs that follow this model:

achiguarse, aguar, amenguar, amortiguar, apaciguar, atestiguar, atreguar, chaguar, desaguar, desambiguar, deslenguarse, fraguar, menguar, santiguar, tameguar

17. bendecir (to bless)

PRESENT	PRESENT SUBJUNCTIVE
bendigo	**bendig**a
bendices	**bendig**as
bendice	**bendig**a
bendecimos	**bendig**amos
bendecís	**bendig**áis
bendicen	**bendig**an

IMPERFECT	IMPERFECT SUBJUNCTIVE
bendecía	**bendijera/bendijese**
bendecías	**bendijeras/bendijeses**
bendecía	**bendijera/bendijese**
bendecíamos	**bendijéramos/bendijésemos**
bendecíais	**bendijerais/bendijeseis**
bendecían	**bendijeran/bendijesen**

FUTURE	CONDITIONAL
bendeciré	bendeciría
bendecirás	bendecirías
bendecirá	bendeciría
bendeciremos	bendeciríamos
bendeciréis	bendeciríais
bendecirán	bendecirían

PRETERITE	IMPERATIVE
bendije	**bendic**e, bendecid
bendijiste	
bendijo	GERUND
bendijimos	**bendic**iendo
bendijisteis	
bendijeron	PAST PARTICIPLE
	bendecido/**bendito**

Other verbs that follow this model:
maldecir

18. caber (to fit)

PRESENT
quepo
cabes
cabe
cabemos
cabéis
caben

PRESENT SUBJUNCTIVE
quepa
quepas
quepa
quepamos
quepáis
quepan

IMPERFECT
cabía
cabías
cabía
cabíamos
cabíais
cabían

IMPERFECT SUBJUNCTIVE
cupiera/**cup**iese
cupieras/**cup**ieses
cupiera/**cup**iese
cupiéramos/**cup**iésemos
cupierais/**cup**ieseis
cupieran/**cup**iesen

FUTURE
cabré
cabrás
cabrá
cabremos
cabréis
cabrán

CONDITIONAL
cabría
cabrías
cabría
cabríamos
cabríais
cabrían

PRETERITE
cupe
cupiste
cupo
cupimos
cupisteis
cupieron

IMPERATIVE
cabe, cabed

GERUND
cabiendo

PAST PARTICIPLE
cabido

19. caer (to fall)

PRESENT	PRESENT SUBJUNCTIVE
caigo	**caig**a
caes	**caig**as
cae	**caig**a
caemos	**caig**amos
caéis	**caig**áis
caen	**caig**an

IMPERFECT	IMPERFECT SUBJUNCTIVE
caía	ca**yera**/ca**yese**
caías	ca**yeras**/ca**yeses**
caía	ca**yera**/ca**yese**
caíamos	ca**yéramos**/ca**yésemos**
caíais	ca**yerais**/ca**yeseis**
caían	ca**yeran**/ca**yesen**

FUTURE	CONDITIONAL
caeré	caería
caerás	caerías
caerá	caería
caeremos	caeríamos
caeréis	caeríais
caerán	caerían

PRETERITE	IMPERATIVE
caí	cae, caed
ca**íste**	
ca**yó**	GERUND
ca**ímos**	ca**yendo**
ca**ísteis**	
ca**yeron**	PAST PARTICIPLE
	caído

Other verbs that follow this model:
decaer, recaer

20. cocer (to boil)

PRESENT	PRESENT SUBJUNCTIVE
cuezo	**cuez**a
cueces	**cuez**as
cuece	**cuez**a
cocemos	**coz**amos
cocéis	**coz**áis
cuecen	**cuez**an

IMPERFECT	IMPERFECT SUBJUNCTIVE
cocía	cociera/cociese
cocías	cocieras/cocieses
cocía	cociera/cociese
cocíamos	cociéramos/cociésemos
cocíais	cocierais/cocieseis
cocían	cocieran/cociesen

FUTURE	CONDITIONAL
coceré	cocería
cocerás	cocerías
cocerá	cocería
coceremos	coceríamos
coceréis	coceríais
cocerán	cocerían

PRETERITE	IMPERATIVE
cocí	**cuec**e, coced
cociste	
coció	GERUND
cocimos	cociendo
cocisteis	
cocieron	PAST PARTICIPLE
	cocido/**cocho**

Other verbs that follow this model:
contorcerse, destorcer, escocer, recocer, retorcer, torcer

21. coger (to catch)

PRESENT	PRESENT SUBJUNCTIVE
cojo	**coj**a
coges	**coj**as
coge	**coj**a
cogemos	**coj**amos
cogéis	**coj**áis
cogen	**coj**an

IMPERFECT	IMPERFECT SUBJUNCTIVE
cogía	cogiera/cogiese
cogías	cogieras/cogieses
cogía	cogiera/cogiese
cogíamos	cogiéramos/cogiésemos
cogíais	cogierais/cogieseis
cogían	cogieran/cogiesen

FUTURE	CONDITIONAL
cogeré	cogería
cogerás	cogerías
cogerá	cogería
cogeremos	cogeríamos
cogeréis	cogeríais
cogerán	cogerían

PRETERITE	IMPERATIVE
cogí	coge, coged
cogiste	
cogió	GERUND
cogimos	cogiendo
cogisteis	
cogieron	PAST PARTICIPLE
	cogido

Other verbs that follow this model:
absterger, acoger, antecoger, asperger, autoprotegerse,
converger, descoger, desencoger, desproteger, deterger,

emerger, encoger, entrecoger, escoger, preescoger, proteger, recoger, sobrecoger, sobreproteger

22. conducir (to drive)

PRESENT	PRESENT SUBJUNCTIVE
conduzco	**conduzc**a
conduces	**conduzc**as
conduce	**conduzc**a
conducimos	**conduzc**amos
conducís	**conduzc**áis
conducen	**conduzc**an

IMPERFECT	IMPERFECT SUBJUNCTIVE
conducía	**condujera/condujese**
conducías	**condujeras/condujeses**
conducía	**condujera/condujese**
conducíamos	**condujéramos/condujésemos**
conducíais	**condujerais/condujeseis**
conducían	**condujeran/condujesen**

FUTURE	CONDITIONAL
conduciré	conduciría
conducirás	conducirías
conducirá	conduciría
conduciremos	conduciríamos
conduciréis	conduciríais
conducirán	conducirían

PRETERITE	IMPERATIVE
conduje	conduce, conducid
condujiste	
condujo	GERUND
condujimos	conduciendo
condujisteis	
condujeron	PAST PARTICIPLE
	conducido

Other verbs that follow this model:
aducir, coproducir, deducir, inducir, introducir, producir, reconducir, reducir, reproducir, seducir, traducir

23. construir (to build)

PRESENT	PRESENT SUBJUNCTIVE
construyo	**construya**
construyes	**construyas**
construye	**construya**
construimos	**construyamos**
construís	**construyáis**
construyen	**construyan**

IMPERFECT	IMPERFECT SUBJUNCTIVE
construía	**construyera/construyese**
construías	**construyeras/construyeses**
construía	**construyera/construyese**
construíamos	**construyéramos/construyésemos**
construíais	**construyerais/construyeseis**
construían	**construyeran/construyesen**

FUTURE	CONDITIONAL
construiré	construiría
construirás	construirías
construirá	construiría
construiremos	construiríamos
construiréis	construiríais
construirán	construirían

PRETERITE	IMPERATIVE
construí	**construy**e, construid
construiste	
construyó	GERUND
construimos	constru**yendo**
construisteis	
construyeron	PAST PARTICIPLE
	construido

Other verbs that follow this model:
afluir, atribuir, autodestruirse, circuir, concluir, confluir,
constituir, contribuir, derruir, desobstruir, destituir, destruir,

Verb Tables

desvaír, diluir, disminuir, distribuir, efluir, estatuir, excluir,
fluir, gruir, huir, imbuir, incluir, influir, inmiscuirse, instituir,
instruir, intuir, luir, obstruir, ocluir, prostituir, recluir,
reconstituir, reconstruir, redistribuir, refluir, restituir,
retribuir, substituir, sustituir

24. contar (to count)

PRESENT	PRESENT SUBJUNCTIVE
cuento	**cuent**e
cuentas	**cuent**es
cuenta	**cuent**e
contamos	contemos
contáis	contéis
cuentan	**cuent**en

IMPERFECT	IMPERFECT SUBJUNCTIVE
contaba	contara/contase
contabas	contaras/contases
contaba	contara/contase
contábamos	contáramos/contásemos
contabais	contarais/contaseis
contaban	contaran/contasen

FUTURE	CONDITIONAL
contaré	contaría
contarás	contarías
contará	contaría
contaremos	contaríamos
contaréis	contaríais
contarán	contarían

PRETERITE	IMPERATIVE
conté	**cuent**a, contad
contaste	
contó	GERUND
contamos	contando
contasteis	
contaron	PAST PARTICIPLE
	contado

Other verbs that follow this model:
acordar, acostar, afollarse, aforar, amoblar, amolar, apostar, aprobar, asolar, asonar, atronar, colar, comprobar, concordar,

consolar, consonar, costar, demostrar, denostar, desacordar, desaforar, desaprobar, descollar, desconsolar, descontar, descornar, desencontrarse, desolar, desollar, despoblar, discordar, disonar, encontrar, encorar, encordar, engrosar, escornar, hollar, improbar, mancornar, mostrar, percollar, poblar, preacordar, probar, recontar, recordar, recostar, reencontrar, renovar, repoblar, reprobar, rescontrar, resollar, resonar, retostar, revolar, rodar, sobrevolar, solar, soldar, soltar, sonar, soñar, superpoblar, tostar, trascolar, trascordarse, trasvolar, tronar, volar

25. crecer (to grow)

PRESENT	PRESENT SUBJUNCTIVE
crezco	**crezc**a
creces	**crezc**as
crece	**crezc**a
crecemos	**crezc**amos
crecéis	**crezc**áis
crecen	**crezc**an

IMPERFECT	IMPERFECT SUBJUNCTIVE
crecía	creciera/creciese
crecías	crecieras/crecieses
crecía	creciera/creciese
crecíamos	creciéramos/creciésemos
crecíais	crecierais/crecieseis
crecían	crecieran/creciesen

FUTURE	CONDITIONAL
creceré	crecería
crecerás	crecerías
crecerá	crecería
creceremos	creceríamos
creceréis	creceríais
crecerán	crecerían

PRETERITE	IMPERATIVE
crecí	crece, creced
creciste	
creció	GERUND
crecimos	creciendo
crecisteis	
crecieron	PAST PARTICIPLE
	crecido

Other verbs that follow this model:
abastecer, aborrecer, acaecer, acontecer, acrecer, adolecer,
adormecer, agradecer, amanecer, anochecer, aparecer,

apetecer, atardecer, autoabastecerse, blanquecer, carecer, compadecer, comparecer, conocer, convalecer, decrecer, desabastecer, desagradecer, desaparecer, desconocer, desentumecer, desfallecer, desfavorecer, desguarnecer, desmerecer, desobedecer, desvanecer, embastecer, embebecer, embellecer, embravecer, embrutecer, empalidecer, empequeñecer, emplastecer, empobrecer, enaltecer, enardecer, encallecer, encanecer, encarecer, enceguecer, endurecer, enflaquecer, enfurecer, engrandecer, enloquecer, enmohecer, enmudecer, ennegrecer, ennoblecer, enorgullecer, enrarecer, enriquecer, enrojecer, enronquecer, ensoberbecer, ensombrecer, ensordecer, entallecer, enternecer, entontecer, entorpecer, entristecer, entullecer, entumecer, envanecer, envejecer, envilecer, escarnecer, esclarecer, establecer, estremecer, fallecer, favorecer, fenecer, florecer, fortalecer, guarecer, guarnecer, humedecer, languidecer, merecer, obedecer, obscurecer, ofrecer, oscurecer, pacer, padecer, palidecer, parecer, perecer, permanecer, pertenecer, prevalecer, reaparecer, reblandecer, reconocer, recrudecer, rejuvenecer, resplandecer, restablecer, reverdecer, robustecer, tardecer, verdecer

26. cruzar (to cross)

PRESENT	PRESENT SUBJUNCTIVE
cruzo	**cruce**
cruzas	**cruces**
cruza	**cruce**
cruzamos	**cruce**mos
cruzáis	**cruc**éis
cruzan	**cruc**en

IMPERFECT	IMPERFECT SUBJUNCTIVE
cruzaba	cruzara/cruzase
cruzabas	cruzaras/cruzases
cruzaba	cruzara/cruzase
cruzábamos	cruzáramos/cruzásemos
cruzabais	cruzarais/cruzaseis
cruzaban	cruzaran/cruzasen

FUTURE	CONDITIONAL
cruzaré	cruzaría
cruzarás	cruzarías
cruzará	cruzaría
cruzaremos	cruzaríamos
cruzaréis	cruzaríais
cruzarán	cruzarían

PRETERITE	IMPERATIVE
crucé	cruza, cruzad
cruzaste	
cruzó	GERUND
cruzamos	cruzando
cruzasteis	
cruzaron	PAST PARTICIPLE
	cruzado

Other verbs that follow this model:
abalanzarse, abanderizar, abonanzar, abrazar, absolutizar,
acezar, acorazar, actualizar, acuatizar, adelgazar, aderezar,

adverbializar, afianzar, africanizar, agilizar, agonizar,
agrazar, aguazar, agudizar, aguzar, alborozar, alcalinizar,
alcanzar, alcoholizar, aleatorizar, alegorizar, alfabetizar,
almohazar, alunizar, aluzar, alzar, amarizar, amenazar,
amenizar, americanizar, amerizar, amordazar, amortizar,
amostazar, analizar, anarquizar, anatematizar, anatomizar,
animalizar, antipatizar, apelmazar, aplazar, arabizar,
armonizar, aromatizar, arrebozar, arregazar, arrizar,
artificializar, atemorizar, atenazar, aterrizar, aterrorizar,
atezar, atizar, atomizar, automatizar, autorizar, avanzar,
avezar, azuzar, banalizar, barnizar, bautizar, bostezar, brezar,
brutalizar, burocratizar, calzar, canalizar, candidatizar,
canonizar, caotizar, capitalizar, caracterizar, caramelizar,
carbonizar, caricaturizar, castellanizar, catalizar, categorizar,
catequizar, cauterizar, cazar, centralizar, chabacanizar,
chapuzar, chuzar, cicatrizar, civilizar, climatizar, colectivizar,
colonizar, comercializar, compatibilizar, computadorizar,
computarizar, computerizar, comunizar, conceptualizar,
concretizar, confraternizar, connaturalizarse, contabilizar,
contemporizar, contextualizar, corporeizar, cotizar,
criminalizar, criogenizar, cristalizar, cristianizar, critiquizar,
culpabilizar, culturizar, danzar, decimalizar, democratizar,
derechizar, desacralizar, desalinizar, desamortizar,
desarmonizar, desautorizar, desbrozar, desburocratizar,
descabezar, descalzar, descapitalizar, descarozar,
descentralizar, descolonizar, descontextualizar, descortezar,
descruzar, descuartizar, desculpabilizar, desdramatizar,
desembarazar, desenlazar, desentronizar, desertizar,
desesperanzar, desestabilizar, desfiscalizar, desguazar,
deshechizar, deshumanizar, desindustrializar, deslegalizar,
deslizar, desmenuzar, desmilitarizar, desmineralizarse,
desmonetizar, desmoralizar, desmovilizar, desnacionalizar,
desnaturalizar, desodorizar, desolidarizarse, desorganizar,
despedazar, despenalizar, desperezarse, despersonalizar,
despolitizar, despiezar, desplazar, despotizar, desratizar,
desregular, desrizar, destazar, destrenzar, destrozar,
desvalorizar, desvitalizar, digitalizar, dinamizar, disfrazar,
divinizar, dogmatizar, dramatizar, ecologizar, economizar,

ecualizar, editorializar, ejemplarizar, electrizar, embarazar,
embarnizar, embazar, embozar, empapuzar, emplazar,
enaguazar, encabezar, encarnizar, encauzar, encolerizar,
enderezar, endulzar, energizar, enfatizar, enfervorizar,
engarzar, enjaezar, enlazar, enlodazar, enrazar, enrizar,
ensalzar, entapizar, entrecruzar, entrelazar, entronizar,
enzarzar, erizar, erotizar, esbozar, escandalizar, esclavizar,
escolarizar, escrupulizar, esguazar, españolizar, especializar,
esperanzar, espiritualizar, esponsorizar, esquematizar,
estabilizar, estandarizar, estatalizar, estatizar, esterilizar,
estigmatizar, estilizar, eternizar, euforizar, evangelizar,
evaporizar, exorcizar, exteriorizar, externalizar, familiarizar,
fanatizar, fecundizar, federalizar, fertilizar, fervorizar,
finalizar, fiscalizar, flexibilizar, focalizar, formalizar,
fosilizarse, fraternizar, frezar, frivolizar, galvanizar,
garantizar, generalizar, germanizar, globalizar, gozar,
granizar, guionizar, hechizar, helenizar, hermetizar,
hibridizar, hidrolizar, higienizar, hipnotizar, hipotetizar,
hispanizar, histerizarse, homogeneizar, horrorizar,
hospitalizar, hostilizar, hozar, humanizar, idealizar, idiotizar,
ilegalizar, ilegitimizar, imbecilizar, impermeabilizar,
indemnizar, independizar, individualizar, indizar,
industrializar, inestabilizar, infantilizar, informatizar,
infrautilizar, inicializar, inmortalizar, inmovilizar, inmunizar,
insensibilizar, insonorizar, institucionalizar, instrumentalizar,
intelectualizar, interiorizar, internacionalizar, internalizar,
intranquilizar, inutilizar, ionizar, ironizar, islamizar, itemizar,
izar, jerarquizar, labializar, laicizar, lanzar, lateralizar,
latinizar, lazar, legalizar, lexicalizar, liberalizar, liofilizar,
localizar, lotizar, macizar, magnetizar, maquinizar,
marginalizar, martirizar, masculinizar, materializar, matizar,
maximizar, mecanizar, mediatizar, memorizar, mentalizar,
mercantilizar, mesmerizar, mestizar, metabolizar, metalizar,
meteorizar, mexicanizar, militarizar, mimetizar, mineralizar,
miniaturizar, minimalizar, minimizar, minusvalorizar,
modernizar, monetizar, monitorizar, monopolizar, moralizar,
motorizar, movilizar, municipalizar, nacionalizar, narcotizar,
nasalizar, naturalizar, nebulizar, negativizar, neutralizar,

nobilizar, nominalizar, normalizar, nuclearizar, obstaculizar, occidentalizar, oficializar, operativizar, optimizar, organizar, orientalizar, orzar, paganizar, palatalizar, panoramizar, parabolizar, paralizar, particularizar, pasterizar, pasteurizar, patentizar, patronizar, pauperizar, penalizar, perennizar, permeabilizar, personalizar, pinzar, pluralizar, poetizar, polarizar, polemizar, polinizar, politizar, popularizar, pormenorizar, potabilizar, preconizar, presurizar, priorizar, privatizar, problematizar, profesionalizar, profetizar, profundizar, protagonizar, psicoanalizar, pulverizar, puntualizar, punzar, quimerizar, racionalizar, radicalizar, ralentizar, realizar, realzar, rebautizar, rebozar, rechazar, reemplazar, regularizar, reinicializar, relanzar, relativizar, remozar, remplazar, rentabilizar, reorganizar, repentizar, reprivatizar, responsabilizar, retozar, reutilizar, revalorizar, revitalizar, rezar, ridiculizar, rivalizar, rizar, robotizar, romanizar, ronzar, rozar, ruborizar, rutinizarse, sacralizar, salinizar, satanizar, satirizar, secularizar, señalizar, sensacionalizar, sensibilizar, serializar, simetrizar, simbolizar, simpatizar, sincronizar, sindicalizar, singularizar, sinterizar, sintetizar, sintomatizar, sintonizar, sistematizar, sobrealzar, socializar, sodomizar, solazar, solemnizar, solidarizar, sollozar, somatizar, sonorizar, sponsorizar, suavizar, sutilizar, tamizar, tapizar, tazar, teatralizar, temporalizar, temporizar, teorizar, tiranizar, tizar, totalizar, tranquilizar, traumatizar, trazar, trenzar, trivializar, trizar, tronzar, uniformizar, universalizar, uperizar, urbanizar, utilizar, valorizar, vampirizar, vaporizar, vehiculizar, velarizar, verbalizar, viabilizar, victimizar, vigorizar, virilizar, visibilizar, visualizar, vitalizar, vocalizar, volatilizar, vulcanizar, vulgarizar

27. dar (to give)

PRESENT
doy
das
da
damos
dais
dan

PRESENT SUBJUNCTIVE
dé
des
dé
demos
deis
den

IMPERFECT
daba
dabas
daba
dábamos
dabais
daban

IMPERFECT SUBJUNCTIVE
diera/diese
dieras/dieses
diera/diese
diéramos/diésemos
dierais/dieseis
dieran/diesen

FUTURE
daré
darás
dará
daremos
daréis
darán

CONDITIONAL
daría
darías
daría
daríamos
daríais
darían

PRETERITE
di
diste
dio
dimos
disteis
dieron

IMPERATIVE
da, dad

GERUND
dando

PAST PARTICIPLE
dado

28. decir (to say)

PRESENT	PRESENT SUBJUNCTIVE
digo	**dig**a
dices	**dig**as
dice	**dig**a
decimos	**dig**amos
decís	**dig**áis
dicen	**dig**an

IMPERFECT	IMPERFECT SUBJUNCTIVE
decía	**dijera/dijese**
decías	**dijeras/dijeses**
decía	**dijera/dijese**
decíamos	**dijéramos/dijésemos**
decíais	**dijerais/dijeseis**
decían	**dijeran/dijesen**

FUTURE	CONDITIONAL
diré	**dir**ía
dirás	**dir**ías
dirá	**dir**ía
diremos	**dir**íamos
diréis	**dir**íais
dirán	**dir**ían

PRETERITE	IMPERATIVE
dije	**di**, decid
dijiste	
dijo	GERUND
dijimos	**dic**iendo
dijisteis	
dijeron	PAST PARTICIPLE
	dicho

Other verbs that follow this model:
contradecir, desdecir, interdecir, predecir

29. degollar (to cut the throat of)

PRESENT	PRESENT SUBJUNCTIVE
degüello	**degüell**e
degüellas	**degüell**es
degüella	**degüell**e
degollamos	degollemos
degolláis	degolléis
degüellan	**degüell**en

IMPERFECT	IMPERFECT SUBJUNCTIVE
degollaba	degollara/degollase
degollabas	degollaras/degollases
degollaba	degollara/degollase
degollábamos	degolláramos/degollásemos
degollabais	degollarais/degollaseis
degollaban	degollaran/degollasen

FUTURE	CONDITIONAL
degollaré	degollaría
degollarás	degollarías
degollará	degollaría
degollaremos	degollaríamos
degollaréis	degollaríais
degollarán	degollarían

PRETERITE	IMPERATIVE
degollé	**degüell**a, degollad
degollaste	
degolló	GERUND
degollamos	degollando
degollasteis	
degollaron	PAST PARTICIPLE
	degollado

Other verbs that follow this model:
regoldar

30. delinquir (to commit a criminal offense)

PRESENT	PRESENT SUBJUNCTIVE
delinco	**delinc**a
delinques	**delinc**as
delinque	**delinc**a
delinquimos	**delinc**amos
delinquís	**delinc**áis
delinquen	**delinc**an

IMPERFECT	IMPERFECT SUBJUNCTIVE
delinquía	delinquiera/delinquiese
delinquías	delinquieras/delinquieses
delinquía	delinquiera/delinquiese
delinquíamos	delinquiéramos/delinquiésemos
delinquíais	delinquierais/delinquieseis
delinquían	delinquieran/delinquiesen

FUTURE	CONDITIONAL
delinquiré	delinquiría
delinquirás	delinquirías
delinquirá	delinquiría
delinquiremos	delinquiríamos
delinquiréis	delinquiríais
delinquirán	delinquirían

PRETERITE	IMPERATIVE
delinquí	delinque, delinquid
delinquiste	
delinquió	GERUND
delinquimos	delinquiendo
delinquisteis	
delinquieron	PAST PARTICIPLE
	delinquido

31. desosar (to pit, to bone, to stone)

PRESENT	PRESENT SUBJUNCTIVE
deshueso	**deshuese**
deshuesas	**deshueses**
deshuesa	**deshuese**
desosamos	desosemos
desosáis	desoséis
deshuesan	**deshuesen**

IMPERFECT	IMPERFECT SUBJUNCTIVE
desosaba	desosara/desosase
desosabas	desosaras/desosases
desosaba	desosara/desosase
desosábamos	desosáramos/desosásemos
desosabais	desosarais/desosaseis
desosaban	desosaran/desosasen

FUTURE	CONDITIONAL
desosaré	desosaría
desosarás	desosarías
desosará	desosaría
desosaremos	desosaríamos
desosaréis	desosaríais
desosarán	desosarían

PRETERITE	IMPERATIVE
desosé	**deshuesa**, desosad
desosaste	
desosó	GERUND
desosamos	desosando
desosasteis	
desosaron	PAST PARTICIPLE
	desosado

32. dirigir (to direct)

PRESENT	PRESENT SUBJUNCTIVE
dirijo	**diri**ja
diriges	**diri**jas
dirige	**diri**ja
dirigimos	**diri**jamos
dirigís	**diri**jáis
dirigen	**diri**jan

IMPERFECT	IMPERFECT SUBJUNCTIVE
dirigía	dirigiera/dirigiese
dirigías	dirigieras/dirigieses
dirigía	dirigiera/dirigiese
dirigíamos	dirigiéramos/dirigiésemos
dirigíais	dirigierais/dirigieseis
dirigían	dirigieran/dirigiesen

FUTURE	CONDITIONAL
dirigiré	dirigiría
dirigirás	dirigirías
dirigirá	dirigiría
dirigiremos	dirigiríamos
dirigiréis	dirigiríais
dirigirán	dirigirían

PRETERITE	IMPERATIVE
dirigí	dirige, dirigid
dirigiste	
dirigió	GERUND
dirigimos	dirigiendo
dirigisteis	
dirigieron	PAST PARTICIPLE
	dirigido

Other verbs that follow this model:
afligir, astringir, atingir, codirigir, compungir, convergir, divergir, erigir, exigir, fingir, fulgir, fungir, infligir, infringir,

inmergir, mugir, pungir, refringir, refulgir, restringir, resurgir, rugir, sumergir, surgir, teledirigir, transigir, ungir, urgir

33. discernir (to discern)

PRESENT
discierno
disciernes
discierne
discernimos
discernís
disciernen

PRESENT SUBJUNCTIVE
discierna
disciernas
discierna
discernamos
discernáis
disciernan

IMPERFECT
discernía
discernías
discernía
discerníamos
discerníais
discernían

IMPERFECT SUBJUNCTIVE
discerniera/discerniese
discernieras/discernieses
discerniera/discerniese
discerniéramos/discerniésemos
discernierais/discernieseis
discernieran/discerniesen

FUTURE
discerniré
discernirás
discernirá
discerniremos
discerniréis
discernirán

CONDITIONAL
discerniría
discernirías
discerniría
discerniríamos
discerniríais
discernirían

PRETERITE
discerní
discerniste
discernió
discernimos
discernisteis
discernieron

IMPERATIVE
discierne, discernid

GERUND
discerniendo

PAST PARTICIPLE
discernido

Other verbs that follow this model:
cernir, concernir, hendir

34. distinguir (to distinguish)

PRESENT	PRESENT SUBJUNCTIVE
distingo	**disting**a
distingues	**disting**as
distingue	**disting**a
distinguimos	**disting**amos
distinguís	**disting**áis
distinguen	**disting**an

IMPERFECT	IMPERFECT SUBJUNCTIVE
distinguía	distinguiera/distinguiese
distinguías	distinguieras/distinguieses
distinguía	distinguiera/distinguiese
distinguíamos	distinguiéramos/distinguiésemos
distinguíais	distinguierais/distinguieseis
distinguían	distinguieran/distinguiesen

FUTURE	CONDITIONAL
distinguiré	distinguiría
distinguirás	distinguirías
distinguirá	distinguiría
distinguiremos	distinguiríamos
distinguiréis	distinguiríais
distinguirán	distinguirían

PRETERITE	IMPERATIVE
distinguí	distingue, distinguid
distinguiste	
distinguió	GERUND
distinguimos	distinguiendo
distinguisteis	
distinguieron	PAST PARTICIPLE
	distinguido

Other verbs that follow this model:
extinguir

45

35. dormir (to sleep)

PRESENT	PRESENT SUBJUNCTIVE
duermo	**duerm**a
duermes	**duerm**as
duerme	**duerm**a
dormimos	**durm**amos
dormís	**durm**áis
duermen	**duerm**an

IMPERFECT	IMPERFECT SUBJUNCTIVE
dormía	**durm**iera/**durm**iese
dormías	**durm**ieras/**durm**ieses
dormía	**durm**iera/**durm**iese
dormíamos	**durm**iéramos/**durm**iésemos
dormíais	**durm**ierais/**durm**ieseis
dormían	**durm**ieran/**durm**iesen

FUTURE	CONDITIONAL
dormiré	dormiría
dormirás	dormirías
dormirá	dormiría
dormiremos	dormiríamos
dormiréis	dormiríais
dormirán	dormirían

PRETERITE	IMPERATIVE
dormí	**duerm**e, dormid
dormiste	
durmió	GERUND
dormimos	**durm**iendo
dormisteis	
durmieron	PAST PARTICIPLE
	dormido

36. elegir (to choose, to elect)

PRESENT
elijo
eliges
elige
eleg**imos**
eleg**ís**
eligen

PRESENT SUBJUNCTIVE
elija
elijas
elija
elijamos
elijáis
elijan

IMPERFECT
eleg**ía**
eleg**ías**
eleg**ía**
eleg**íamos**
eleg**íais**
eleg**ían**

IMPERFECT SUBJUNCTIVE
eligiera/**elig**iese
eligieras/**elig**ieses
eligiera/**elig**iese
eligiéramos/**elig**iésemos
eligierais/**elig**ieseis
eligieran/**elig**iesen

FUTURE
elegir**é**
elegir**ás**
elegir**á**
elegir**emos**
elegir**éis**
elegir**án**

CONDITIONAL
elegir**ía**
elegir**ías**
elegir**ía**
elegir**íamos**
elegir**íais**
elegir**ían**

PRETERITE
eleg**í**
eleg**iste**
eligió
eleg**imos**
eleg**isteis**
eligieron

IMPERATIVE
elige, eleg**id**

GERUND
eligiendo

PAST PARTICIPLE
eleg**ido**/**electo**

Other verbs that follow this model:
colegir, corregir, reelegir, regir

37. embaír (to deceive)

PRESENT	PRESENT SUBJUNCTIVE
-	-
-	-
-	-
emba**ímos**	-
emba**ís**	-
-	-

IMPERFECT	IMPERFECT SUBJUNCTIVE
emba**ía**	emba**yera**/emba**yese**
emba**ías**	emba**yeras**/emba**yeses**
emba**ía**	emba**yera**/emba**yese**
emba**íamos**	emba**yéramos**/emba**yésemos**
emba**íais**	emba**yerais**/emba**yeseis**
emba**ían**	emba**yeran**/emba**yesen**

FUTURE	CONDITIONAL
embairé	**embair**ía
embairás	**embair**ías
embairá	**embair**ía
embairemos	**embair**íamos
embairéis	**embair**íais
embairán	**embair**ían

PRETERITE	IMPERATIVE
emba**í**	-, emba**íd**
emba**íste**	
emba**yó**	GERUND
emba**ímos**	emba**yendo**
emba**ísteis**	
emba**yeron**	PAST PARTICIPLE
	emba**ído**

38. empezar (to begin)

PRESENT	PRESENT SUBJUNCTIVE
empiezo	**empiec**e
empiezas	**empiec**es
empieza	**empiec**e
empezamos	**empec**emos
empezáis	**empec**éis
empiezan	**empiec**en

IMPERFECT	IMPERFECT SUBJUNCTIVE
empezaba	empezara/empezase
empezabas	empezaras/empezases
empezaba	empezara/empezase
empezábamos	empezáramos/empezásemos
empezabais	empezarais/empezaseis
empezaban	empezaran/empezasen

FUTURE	CONDITIONAL
empezaré	empezaría
empezarás	empezarías
empezará	empezaría
empezaremos	empezaríamos
empezaréis	empezaríais
empezarán	empezarían

PRETERITE	IMPERATIVE
empecé	**empiez**a, empezad
empezaste	
empezó	GERUND
empezamos	empezando
empezasteis	
empezaron	PAST PARTICIPLE
	empezado

Other verbs that follow this model:
comenzar, recomenzar, tropezar

39. enraizar (to take root)

PRESENT	PRESENT SUBJUNCTIVE
enraízo	**enraíc**e
enraízas	**enraíc**es
enraíza	**enraíc**e
enraizamos	**enraic**emos
enraizáis	**enraic**éis
enraízan	**enraíc**en

IMPERFECT	IMPERFECT SUBJUNCTIVE
enraizaba	enraizara/enraizase
enraizabas	enraizaras/enraizases
enraizaba	enraizara/enraizase
enraizábamos	enraizáramos/enraizásemos
enraizabais	enraizarais/enraizaseis
enraizaban	enraizaran/enraizasen

FUTURE	CONDITIONAL
enraizaré	enraizaría
enraizarás	enraizarías
enraizará	enraizaría
enraizaremos	enraizaríamos
enraizaréis	enraizaríais
enraizarán	enraizarían

PRETERITE	IMPERATIVE
enraicé	**enraíz**a, enraizad
enraizaste	
enraizó	GERUND
enraizamos	enraizando
enraizasteis	
enraizaron	PAST PARTICIPLE
	enraizado

Other verbs that follow this model:
arcaizar, europeizar, hebraizar, judaizar

40. entender (to understand)

PRESENT	PRESENT SUBJUNCTIVE
entiendo	**entiend**a
entiendes	**entiend**as
entiende	**entiend**a
entendemos	entendamos
entendéis	entendáis
entienden	**entiend**an

IMPERFECT	IMPERFECT SUBJUNCTIVE
entendía	entendiera/entendiese
entendías	entendieras/entendieses
entendía	entendiera/entendiese
entendíamos	entendiéramos/entendiésemos
entendíais	entendierais/entendieseis
entendían	entendieran/entendiesen

FUTURE	CONDITIONAL
entenderé	entendería
entenderás	entenderías
entenderá	entendería
entenderemos	entenderíamos
entenderéis	entenderíais
entenderán	entenderían

PRETERITE	IMPERATIVE
entendí	**entiend**e, entended
entendiste	
entendió	GERUND
entendimos	entendiendo
entendisteis	
entendieron	PAST PARTICIPLE
	entendido

Other verbs that follow this model:
ascender, atender, cerner, condescender, contender, defender, desatender, descender, desentenderse, distender, encender,

Verb Tables

extender, heder, hender, malentender, perder, reencender, reverter, sobreentender, sobrentender, subentender, subtender, superentender, tender, transcender, trascender, trasverter, verter

41. enviar (to send)

PRESENT	PRESENT SUBJUNCTIVE
envío	**envíe**
envías	**enví**es
envía	**envíe**
enviamos	enviemos
enviáis	enviéis
envían	**enví**en

IMPERFECT	IMPERFECT SUBJUNCTIVE
enviaba	enviara/enviase
enviabas	enviaras/enviases
enviaba	enviara/enviase
enviábamos	enviáramos/enviásemos
enviabais	enviarais/enviaseis
enviaban	enviaran/enviasen

FUTURE	CONDITIONAL
enviaré	enviaría
enviarás	enviarías
enviará	enviaría
enviaremos	enviaríamos
enviaréis	enviaríais
enviarán	enviarían

PRETERITE	IMPERATIVE
envié	**enví**a, enviad
enviaste	
envió	GERUND
enviamos	enviando
enviasteis	
enviaron	PAST PARTICIPLE
	enviado

Other verbs that follow this model:
aeroenviar, aliar, amnistiar, ampliar, ansiar, arriar, ataviar, averiar, aviar, biografiar, cablegrafiar, calcografiar,

caligrafiar, chirriar, ciar, confiar, contrariar, coreografiar, criar, desafiar, descarriar, desconfiar, desliar, desvariar, desviar, enfriar, escalofriar, espiar, esquiar, estenografiar, estriar, expatriar, expiar, extasiar, extraviar, fiar, fotografiar, guiar, hastiar, inventariar, liar, malcriar, mecanografiar, piar, porfiar, radiografiar, recriar, reenviar, reliar, repatriar, resfriar, rociar, sumariar, taquigrafiar, telegrafiar, vaciar, variar, vidriar, xerografiar

42. erguir (to erect)

PRESENT
irgo/**yerg**o
irgues/**yergu**es
irgue/**yergu**e
erguimos
erguís
irguen/**yergu**en

PRESENT SUBJUNCTIVE
irga/**yerg**a
irgas/**yerg**as
irga/**yerg**a
irgamos/**yerg**amos
irgáis/**yerg**áis
irgan/**yerg**an

IMPERFECT
erguía
erguías
erguía
erguíamos
erguíais
erguían

IMPERFECT SUBJUNCTIVE
irguiera/**irgu**iese
irguieras/**irgu**ieses
irguiera/**irgu**iese
irguiéramos/**irgu**iésemos
irguierais/**irgu**ieseis
irguieran/**irgu**iesen

FUTURE
erguiré
erguirás
erguirá
erguiremos
erguiréis
erguirán

CONDITIONAL
erguiría
erguirías
erguiría
erguiríamos
erguiríais
erguirían

PRETERITE
erguí
erguiste
irguió
erguimos
erguisteis
irguieron

IMPERATIVE
irgue/**yergu**e, erguid

GERUND
irguiendo

PAST PARTICIPLE
erguido

43. errar (to err)

PRESENT	PRESENT SUBJUNCTIVE
yerro	**yerr**e
yerras	**yerr**es
yerra	**yerr**e
erramos	erremos
erráis	erréis
yerran	**yerr**en

IMPERFECT	IMPERFECT SUBJUNCTIVE
erraba	errara/errase
errabas	erraras/errases
erraba	errara/errase
errábamos	erráramos/errásemos
errabais	errarais/erraseis
erraban	erraran/errasen

FUTURE	CONDITIONAL
erraré	erraría
errarás	errarías
errará	erraría
erraremos	erraríamos
erraréis	erraríais
errarán	errarían

PRETERITE	IMPERATIVE
erré	**yerr**a, errad
erraste	
erró	GERUND
erramos	errando
errasteis	
erraron	PAST PARTICIPLE
	errado

44. escribir (to write)

PRESENT
escribo
escribes
escribe
escribimos
escribís
escriben

PRESENT SUBJUNCTIVE
escriba
escribas
escriba
escribamos
escribáis
escriban

IMPERFECT
escribía
escribías
escribía
escribíamos
escribíais
escribían

IMPERFECT SUBJUNCTIVE
escribiera/escribiese
escribieras/escribieses
escribiera/escribiese
escribiéramos/escribiésemos
escribierais/escribieseis
escribieran/escribiesen

FUTURE
escribiré
escribirás
escribirá
escribiremos
escribiréis
escribirán

CONDITIONAL
escribiría
escribirías
escribiría
escribiríamos
escribiríais
escribirían

PRETERITE
escribí
escribiste
escribió
escribimos
escribisteis
escribieron

IMPERATIVE
escribe, escribid

GERUND
escribiendo

PAST PARTICIPLE
escrito

Other verbs that follow this model:

adscribir, circunscribir, describir, inscribir, prescribir, proscribir, reescribir, sobreescribir, subscribir, suscribir, transcribir

45. estar (to be)

PRESENT	PRESENT SUBJUNCTIVE
est**oy**	est**é**
est**ás**	est**és**
est**á**	est**é**
estamos	estemos
estáis	estéis
est**án**	est**én**

IMPERFECT	IMPERFECT SUBJUNCTIVE
estaba	est**uviera**/est**uviese**
estabas	est**uvieras**/est**uvieses**
estaba	est**uviera**/est**uviese**
estábamos	est**uviéramos**/est**uviésemos**
estabais	est**uvierais**/est**uvieseis**
estaban	est**uvieran**/est**uviesen**

FUTURE	CONDITIONAL
estaré	estaría
estarás	estarías
estará	estaría
estaremos	estaríamos
estaréis	estaríais
estarán	estarían

PRETERITE	IMPERATIVE
est**uve**	est**á**, estad
est**uviste**	
est**uvo**	GERUND
est**uvimos**	estando
est**uvisteis**	
est**uvieron**	PAST PARTICIPLE
	estado

46. freír (to fry)

PRESENT	PRESENT SUBJUNCTIVE
frío	**frí**a
fríes	**frí**as
fríe	**frí**a
fre**ímos**	**fri**amos
fre**ís**	**fri**áis/**friais**
fríen	**frí**an

IMPERFECT	IMPERFECT SUBJUNCTIVE
fre**ía**	**fri**era/**fri**ese
fre**ías**	**fri**eras/**fri**eses
fre**ía**	**fri**era/**fri**ese
fre**íamos**	**fri**éramos/**fri**ésemos
fre**íais**	**fri**erais/**fri**eseis
fre**ían**	**fri**eran/**fri**esen

FUTURE	CONDITIONAL
freiré	**freir**ía
freirás	**freir**ías
freirá	**freir**ía
freiremos	**freir**íamos
freiréis	**freir**íais
freirán	**freir**ían

PRETERITE	IMPERATIVE
fre**í**	**frí**e, fre**íd**
fre**íste**	
frió/**frio**	GERUND
fre**ímos**	**fri**endo
fre**ísteis**	
frieron	PAST PARTICIPLE
	frito

Other verbs that follow this model:
sofreír

47. gruñir (to grumble)

PRESENT	PRESENT SUBJUNCTIVE
gruño	gruña
gruñes	gruñas
gruñe	gruña
gruñimos	gruñamos
gruñís	gruñáis
gruñen	gruñan

IMPERFECT	IMPERFECT SUBJUNCTIVE
gruñía	gruñ**era**/gruñ**ese**
gruñías	gruñ**eras**/gruñ**eses**
gruñía	gruñ**era**/gruñ**ese**
gruñíamos	gruñ**éramos**/gruñ**ésemos**
gruñíais	gruñ**erais**/gruñ**eseis**
gruñían	gruñ**eran**/gruñ**esen**

FUTURE	CONDITIONAL
gruñiré	gruñiría
gruñirás	gruñirías
gruñirá	gruñiría
gruñiremos	gruñiríamos
gruñiréis	gruñiríais
gruñirán	gruñirían

PRETERITE	IMPERATIVE
gruñí	gruñe, gruñid
gruñiste	
gruñ**ó**	GERUND
gruñimos	gruñ**endo**
gruñisteis	
gruñ**eron**	PAST PARTICIPLE
	gruñido

Other verbs that follow this model:
bruñir, bullir, engullir, escabullirse, fallir, gañir, mullir, muñir, plañir, rebullir, retiñir, tullir, zambullir

48. haber (to have (auxiliary verb))

PRESENT	PRESENT SUBJUNCTIVE
he	**hay**a
has	**hay**as
ha/hay (impersonal)	**hay**a
hemos	**hay**amos
habéis	**hay**áis
han	**hay**an

IMPERFECT	IMPERFECT SUBJUNCTIVE
había	**hub**iera/**hub**iese
habías	**hub**ieras/**hub**ieses
había	**hub**iera/**hub**iese
habíamos	**hub**iéramos/**hub**iésemos
habíais	**hub**ierais/**hub**ieseis
habían	**hub**ieran/**hub**iesen

FUTURE	CONDITIONAL
habré	**habr**ía
habrás	**habr**ías
habrá	**habr**ía
habremos	**habr**íamos
habréis	**habr**íais
habrán	**habr**ían

PRETERITE	IMPERATIVE
hube	not used
hubiste	
hubo	GERUND
hubimos	habiendo
hubisteis	
hubieron	PAST PARTICIPLE
	habido

49. hacer (to do, to make)

PRESENT	PRESENT SUBJUNCTIVE
hago	**hag**a
haces	**hag**as
hace	**hag**a
hacemos	**hag**amos
hacéis	**hag**áis
hacen	**hag**an

IMPERFECT	IMPERFECT SUBJUNCTIVE
hacía	**hic**iera/**hic**iese
hacías	**hic**ieras/**hic**ieses
hacía	**hic**iera/**hic**iese
hacíamos	**hic**iéramos/**hic**iésemos
hacíais	**hic**ierais/**hic**ieseis
hacían	**hic**ieran/**hic**iesen

FUTURE	CONDITIONAL
haré	**har**ía
harás	**har**ías
hará	**har**ía
haremos	**har**íamos
haréis	**har**íais
harán	**har**ían

PRETERITE	IMPERATIVE
hice	**haz**, haced
hiciste	
hizo	GERUND
hicimos	haciendo
hicisteis	
hicieron	PAST PARTICIPLE
	hecho

Other verbs that follow this model:
deshacer, satisfacer

50. imprimir (to print)

PRESENT	PRESENT SUBJUNCTIVE
imprimo	imprima
imprimes	imprimas
imprime	imprima
imprimimos	imprimamos
imprimís	imprimáis
imprimen	impriman

IMPERFECT	IMPERFECT SUBJUNCTIVE
imprimía	imprimiera/imprimiese
imprimías	imprimieras/imprimieses
imprimía	imprimiera/imprimiese
imprimíamos	imprimiéramos/imprimiésemos
imprimíais	imprimierais/imprimieseis
imprimían	imprimieran/imprimiesen

FUTURE	CONDITIONAL
imprimiré	imprimiría
imprimirás	imprimirías
imprimirá	imprimiría
imprimiremos	imprimiríamos
imprimiréis	imprimiríais
imprimirán	imprimirían

PRETERITE	IMPERATIVE
imprimí	imprime, imprimid
imprimiste	
imprimió	GERUND
imprimimos	imprimiendo
imprimisteis	
imprimieron	PAST PARTICIPLE
	imprimido/**impreso**

Other verbs that follow this model:
reimprimir

51. ir (to go)

PRESENT	PRESENT SUBJUNCTIVE
voy	**vay**a
vas	**vay**as
va	**vay**a
vamos	**vay**amos
vais	**vay**áis
van	**vay**an

IMPERFECT	IMPERFECT SUBJUNCTIVE
iba	**fuera/fuese**
ibas	**fueras/fueses**
iba	**fuera/fuese**
íbamos	**fuéramos/fuésemos**
ibais	**fuerais/fueseis**
iban	**fueran/fuesen**

FUTURE	CONDITIONAL
iré	iría
irás	irías
irá	iría
iremos	iríamos
iréis	iríais
irán	irían

PRETERITE	IMPERATIVE
fui	**ve**, **id**
fuiste	
fue	GERUND
fuimos	**yendo**
fuisteis	
fueron	PAST PARTICIPLE
	ido

52. jugar (to play)

PRESENT	PRESENT SUBJUNCTIVE
juego	**juegu**e
juegas	**juegu**es
juega	**juegu**e
jugamos	**jugu**emos
jugáis	**jugu**éis
juegan	**juegu**en

IMPERFECT	IMPERFECT SUBJUNCTIVE
jugaba	jugara/jugase
jugabas	jugaras/jugases
jugaba	jugara/jugase
jugábamos	jugáramos/jugásemos
jugabais	jugarais/jugaseis
jugaban	jugaran/jugasen

FUTURE	CONDITIONAL
jugaré	jugaría
jugarás	jugarías
jugará	jugaría
jugaremos	jugaríamos
jugaréis	jugaríais
jugarán	jugarían

PRETERITE	IMPERATIVE
jugué	**jueg**a, jugad
jugaste	
jugó	GERUND
jugamos	jugando
jugasteis	
jugaron	PAST PARTICIPLE
	jugado

53. leer (to read)

PRESENT	PRESENT SUBJUNCTIVE
leo	lea
lees	leas
lee	lea
leemos	leamos
leéis	leáis
leen	lean

IMPERFECT	IMPERFECT SUBJUNCTIVE
leía	le**yera**/le**yese**
leías	le**yeras**/le**yeses**
leía	le**yera**/le**yese**
leíamos	le**yéramos**/le**yésemos**
leíais	le**yerais**/le**yeseis**
leían	le**yeran**/le**yesen**

FUTURE	CONDITIONAL
leeré	leería
leerás	leerías
leerá	leería
leeremos	leeríamos
leeréis	leeríais
leerán	leerían

PRETERITE	IMPERATIVE
leí	lee, leed
le**íste**	
le**yó**	GERUND
le**ímos**	le**yendo**
le**ísteis**	
le**yeron**	PAST PARTICIPLE
	le**ído**

Other verbs that follow this model:
creer, descreer, desposeer, desproveer, peer, poseer, proveer, releer, sobreseer

54. lucir (to shine)

PRESENT	PRESENT SUBJUNCTIVE
luzco	**luzc**a
luces	**luzc**as
luce	**luzc**a
lucimos	**luzc**amos
lucís	**luzc**áis
lucen	**luzc**an

IMPERFECT	IMPERFECT SUBJUNCTIVE
lucía	luciera/luciese
lucías	lucieras/lucieses
lucía	luciera/luciese
lucíamos	luciéramos/luciésemos
lucíais	lucierais/lucieseis
lucían	lucieran/luciesen

FUTURE	CONDITIONAL
luciré	luciría
lucirás	lucirías
lucirá	luciría
luciremos	luciríamos
luciréis	luciríais
lucirán	lucirían

PRETERITE	IMPERATIVE
lucí	luce, lucid
luciste	
lució	GERUND
lucimos	luciendo
lucisteis	
lucieron	PAST PARTICIPLE
	lucido

Other verbs that follow this model:
deslucir, enlucir, entrelucir, relucir, translucirse, traslucir

55. morir (to die)

PRESENT	PRESENT SUBJUNCTIVE
muero	muera
mueres	mueras
muere	muera
morimos	muramos
morís	muráis
mueren	mueran

IMPERFECT	IMPERFECT SUBJUNCTIVE
moría	muriera/muriese
morías	murieras/murieses
moría	muriera/muriese
moríamos	muriéramos/muriésemos
moríais	murierais/murieseis
morían	murieran/muriesen

FUTURE	CONDITIONAL
moriré	moriría
morirás	morirías
morirá	moriría
moriremos	moriríamos
moriréis	moriríais
morirán	morirían

PRETERITE	IMPERATIVE
morí	muere, morid
moriste	
murió	GERUND
morimos	muriendo
moristeis	
murieron	PAST PARTICIPLE
	muerto

56. mover (to move)

PRESENT	PRESENT SUBJUNCTIVE
muevo	**muev**a
mueves	**muev**as
mueve	**muev**a
movemos	movamos
movéis	mováis
mueven	**muev**an

IMPERFECT	IMPERFECT SUBJUNCTIVE
movía	moviera/moviese
movías	movieras/movieses
movía	moviera/moviese
movíamos	moviéramos/moviésemos
movíais	movierais/movieseis
movían	movieran/moviesen

FUTURE	CONDITIONAL
moveré	movería
moverás	moverías
moverá	movería
moveremos	moveríamos
moveréis	moveríais
moverán	moverían

PRETERITE	IMPERATIVE
moví	**muev**e, moved
moviste	
movió	GERUND
movimos	moviendo
movisteis	
movieron	PAST PARTICIPLE
	movido

Other verbs that follow this model:
amover, condolerse, conmover, demoler, doler, llover, moler, morder, promover, remoler, remorder, remover, soler

57. nacer (to be born)

PRESENT	PRESENT SUBJUNCTIVE
nazco	**nazc**a
naces	**nazc**as
nace	**nazc**a
nacemos	**nazc**amos
nacéis	**nazc**áis
nacen	**nazc**an

IMPERFECT	IMPERFECT SUBJUNCTIVE
nacía	naciera/naciese
nacías	nacieras/nacieses
nacía	naciera/naciese
nacíamos	naciéramos/naciésemos
nacíais	nacierais/nacieseis
nacían	nacieran/naciesen

FUTURE	CONDITIONAL
naceré	nacería
nacerás	nacerías
nacerá	nacería
naceremos	naceríamos
naceréis	naceríais
nacerán	nacerían

PRETERITE	IMPERATIVE
nací	nace, naced
naciste	
nació	GERUND
nacimos	naciendo
nacisteis	
nacieron	PAST PARTICIPLE
	nacido/**nado**/**nato**

Other verbs that follow this model:
renacer

58. negar (to deny)

PRESENT	PRESENT SUBJUNCTIVE
niego	**niegu**e
niegas	**niegu**es
niega	**niegu**e
negamos	**negu**emos
negáis	**negu**éis
niegan	**niegu**en

IMPERFECT	IMPERFECT SUBJUNCTIVE
negaba	negara/negase
negabas	negaras/negases
negaba	nagara/negase
negábamos	negáramos/negásemos
negabais	negarais/negaseis
negaban	negaran/negasen

FUTURE	CONDITIONAL
negaré	negaría
negarás	negarías
negará	negaría
negaremos	negaríamos
negaréis	negaríais
negarán	negarían

PRETERITE	IMPERATIVE
negué	**nieg**a, negad
negaste	
negó	GERUND
negamos	negando
negasteis	
negaron	PAST PARTICIPLE
	negado

Other verbs that follow this model:

72

abnegar, cegar, denegar, desasosegar, desplegar, estregar, fregar, plegar, refregar, regar, renegar, replegar, restregar, segar, sosegar, trasegar

59. oír (to hear)

PRESENT	PRESENT SUBJUNCTIVE
oigo	**oig**a
oyes	**oig**as
oye	**oig**a
o**ímos**	**oig**amos
oís	**oig**áis
oyen	**oig**an

IMPERFECT	IMPERFECT SUBJUNCTIVE
oía	o**yera**/o**yese**
oías	o**yeras**/o**yeses**
oía	o**yera**/o**yese**
oíamos	o**yéramos**/o**yésemos**
oíais	o**yerais**/o**yeseis**
oían	o**yeran**/o**yesen**

FUTURE	CONDITIONAL
oiré	**oir**ía
oirás	**oir**ías
oirá	**oir**ía
oiremos	**oir**íamos
oiréis	**oir**íais
oirán	**oir**ían

PRETERITE	IMPERATIVE
oí	**oy**e, o**íd**
o**íste**	
o**yó**	GERUND
o**ímos**	**oyendo**
o**ísteis**	
o**yeron**	PAST PARTICIPLE
	o**ído**

Other verbs that follow this model:
desoír, entreoír, trasoír

60. oler (to smell)

PRESENT	PRESENT SUBJUNCTIVE
huelo	**huel**a
hueles	**huel**as
huele	**huel**a
olemos	olamos
oléis	oláis
huelen	**huel**an

IMPERFECT	IMPERFECT SUBJUNCTIVE
olía	oliera/oliese
olías	olieras/olieses
olía	oliera/oliese
olíamos	oliéramos/oliésemos
olíais	olierais/olieseis
olían	olieran/oliesen

FUTURE	CONDITIONAL
oleré	olería
olerás	olerías
olerá	olería
oleremos	oleríamos
oleréis	oleríais
olerán	olerían

PRETERITE	IMPERATIVE
olí	**huel**e, oled
oliste	
olió	GERUND
olimos	oliendo
olisteis	
olieron	PAST PARTICIPLE
	olido

61. pagar (to pay)

PRESENT	PRESENT SUBJUNCTIVE
pago	**pagu**e
pagas	**pagu**es
paga	**pagu**e
pagamos	**pagu**emos
pagáis	**pagu**éis
pagan	**pagu**en

IMPERFECT	IMPERFECT SUBJUNCTIVE
pagaba	pagara/pagase
pagabas	pagaras/pagases
pagaba	pagara/pagase
pagábamos	pagáramos/pagásemos
pagabais	pagarais/pagaseis
pagaban	pagaran/pagasen

FUTURE	CONDITIONAL
pagaré	pagaría
pagarás	pagarías
pagará	pagaría
pagaremos	pagaríamos
pagaréis	pagaríais
pagarán	pagarían

PRETERITE	IMPERATIVE
pagué	paga, pagad
pagaste	
pagó	GERUND
pagamos	pagando
pagasteis	
pagaron	PAST PARTICIPLE
	pagado/**pago**

Other verbs that follow this model:
abogar, aborregarse, abotagarse, abrigar, abrogar, agregar, agringarse, ahogar, alagarse, alargar, albergar, alechugar,

alegar, aletargar, allegar, amadrigar, amagar, amargar,
amigar, amusgar, anegar, antepagar, añusgar, apagar,
aparragarse, apechugar, apegarse, apersogar, apesgar,
arengar, arraigar, arremangar, arrepanchigarse, arriesgar,
arrogar, arrugar, atafagar, atarragarse, atarugar, atosigar,
azogar, bogar, bregar, cabalgar, cagar, cargar, castigar,
catalogar, centrifugar, changar, chingar, circunnavegar,
coaligar, coligarse, comulgar, congregar, conjugar, delegar,
derogar, derrengar, desabrigar, desahogar, desapegarse,
desarraigar, desarrugar, descabalgar, descargar,
descuajaringar, descuajeringar, desegregar, desembargar,
desembragar, desembriagar, desfogar, desguañangar,
desligar, desmigar, desnarigar, despechugarse, despegar,
desperdigar, desporrondingarse, desvirgar, devengar,
dialogar, diptongar, disgregar, divagar, divulgar, doblegar,
dragar, drogar, embargar, embragar, embriagar, empalagar,
encabalgar, encargar, encenagarse, endilgar, endomingarse,
endrogarse, enfangar, engalgar, enjalbegar, enjuagar, enjugar,
entalegar, entongar, entregar, enyugar, erogar, espigar,
espulgar, estomagar, estragar, excomulgar, expurgar, fatigar,
fisgar, fugarse, fumigar, fustigar, halagar, homologar,
hostigar, hurgar, indagar, instigar, interrogar, intrigar,
investigar, irrigar, irrogar, jalbegar, jeringar, juzgar, largar,
legar, ligar, litigar, llagar, llegar, madrugar, malpagar,
mangar, mendigar, merengar, migar, mingar, mitigar,
monologar, monoptongar, naufragar, navegar, obligar,
otorgar, pegar, pingar, plagar, postergar, prejuzgar, pringar,
prodigar, prologar, prolongar, promulgar, propagar,
prorrogar, purgar, rasgar, recargar, rehogar, relegar,
remangar, repagar, repanchigarse, repantigarse, respingar,
rezagar, rezongar, segregar, sesgar, sirgar, sobrecargar,
sojuzgar, subdelegar, subrogar, subyugar, sufragar, tangar,
tingar, trasigar, telecargar, tragar, vagar, vengar

62. pedir (to ask for)

PRESENT	PRESENT SUBJUNCTIVE
pido	**pid**a
pides	**pid**as
pide	**pid**a
pedimos	**pid**amos
pedís	**pid**áis
piden	**pid**an

IMPERFECT	IMPERFECT SUBJUNCTIVE
pedía	**pid**iera/**pid**iese
pedías	**pid**ieras/**pid**ieses
pedía	**pid**iera/**pid**iese
pedíamos	**pid**iéramos/**pid**iésemos
pedíais	**pid**ierais/**pid**ieseis
pedían	**pid**ieran/**pid**iesen

FUTURE	CONDITIONAL
pediré	pediría
pedirás	pedirías
pedirá	pediría
pediremos	pediríamos
pediréis	pediríais
pedirán	pedirían

PRETERITE	IMPERATIVE
pedí	**pid**e, pedid
pediste	
pidió	GERUND
pedimos	**pid**iendo
pedisteis	
pidieron	PAST PARTICIPLE
	pedido

Other verbs that follow this model:
acomedirse, comedirse, competir, concebir, derretir,
descomedirse, desmedirse, despedir, desvestir, embestir,

Verb Tables

expedir, gemir, henchir, impedir, investir, medir, preconcebir, reexpedir, rendir, repetir, revestir, servir, travestir, vestir

63. pensar (to think)

PRESENT	PRESENT SUBJUNCTIVE
pienso	**piense**
piensas	**pienses**
piensa	**piense**
pensamos	pensemos
penséis	penséis
piensan	**piensen**

IMPERFECT	IMPERFECT SUBJUNCTIVE
pensaba	pensara/pensase
pensabas	pensaras/pensases
pensaba	pensara/pensase
pensábamos	pensáramos/pensásemos
pensabais	pensarais/pensaseis
pensaban	pensaran/pensasen

FUTURE	CONDITIONAL
pensaré	pensaría
pensarás	pensarías
pensará	pensaría
pensaremos	pensaríamos
pensaréis	pensaríais
pensarán	pensarían

PRETERITE	IMPERATIVE
pensé	**piensa**, pensad
pensaste	
pensó	GERUND
pensamos	pensando
pensasteis	
pensaron	PAST PARTICIPLE
	pensado

Other verbs that follow this model:
acertar, acrecentar, alentar, apacentar, apretar, arrendar,
asentar, aserrar, aterrar, atestar, atravesar, aventar, beldar,

Verb Tables

calentar, cerrar, cimentar, concertar, confesar, dentar, desacertar, desalentar, desapretar, desaterrar, desconcertar, desempedrar, desenterrar, desgobernar, deshelar, desherbar, desmembrar, despertar, desterrar, emparentar, empedrar, encentar, encerrar, encomendar, endentar, enhestar, enmelar, enmendar, ensangrentar, enterrar, entesar, entierrar, entrecerrar, escarmentar, gobernar, helar, herrar, incensar, invernar, malpensar, manifestar, melar, mentar, merendar, nevar, precalentar, quebrar, reasentar, recalentar, recomendar, remendar, repensar, requebrar, resquebrar, reventar, salpimentar, sembrar, sentar, serrar, sobrecalentar, soterrar, subarrendar, temblar, tentar

64. placer (to please)

PRESENT	PRESENT SUBJUNCTIVE
plazco	**plazc**a
places	**plazc**as
place	**plazc**a/**pleg**a/**plegue**
placemos	**plazc**amos
placéis	**plazc**áis
placen	**plazc**an

IMPERFECT	IMPERFECT SUBJUNCTIVE
placía	placiera/placiese
placías	placieras/placieses
placía	placiera/**plugu**iera/placiese/**plugu**iese
placíamos	placiéramos/placiésemos
placíais	placierais/placieseis
placían	placieran/**plugu**ieran/placiesen/**plugu**iesen

FUTURE	CONDITIONAL
placeré	placería
placerás	placerías
placerá	placería
placeremos	placeríamos
placeréis	placeríais
placerán	placerían

PRETERITE	IMPERATIVE
plací	place, placed
placiste	
plació/**plugo**	GERUND
placimos	placiendo
placisteis	
placieron/**plugu**ieron	PAST PARTICIPLE
	placido

Other verbs that follow this model:
complacer, desplacer

65. poder (to be able to)

PRESENT
puedo
puedes
puede
podemos
podéis
pueden

PRESENT SUBJUNCTIVE
pueda
puedas
pueda
podamos
podáis
puedan

IMPERFECT
podía
podías
podía
podíamos
podíais
podían

IMPERFECT SUBJUNCTIVE
pudiera/**pud**iese
pudieras/**pud**ieses
pudiera/**pud**iese
pudiéramos/**pud**iésemos
pudierais/**pud**ieseis
pudieran/**pud**iesen

FUTURE
podré
podrás
podrá
podremos
podréis
podrán

CONDITIONAL
podría
podrías
podría
podríamos
podríais
podrían

PRETERITE
pude
pudiste
pudo
pudimos
pudisteis
pudieron

IMPERATIVE
puede, poded

GERUND
pudiendo

PAST PARTICIPLE
podido

66. poner (to put)

PRESENT	PRESENT SUBJUNCTIVE
pongo	**ponga**
pones	**pongas**
pone	**ponga**
ponemos	**pongamos**
ponéis	**pongáis**
ponen	**pongan**

IMPERFECT	IMPERFECT SUBJUNCTIVE
ponía	**pusiera/pusiese**
ponías	**pusieras/pusieses**
ponía	**pusiera/pusiese**
poníamos	**pusiéramos/pusiésemos**
poníais	**pusierais/pusieseis**
ponían	**pusieran/pusiesen**

FUTURE	CONDITIONAL
pondré	**pondría**
pondrás	**pondrías**
pondrá	**pondría**
pondremos	**pondríamos**
pondréis	**pondríais**
pondrán	**pondrían**

PRETERITE	IMPERATIVE
puse	**pon**, poned
pusiste	
puso	GERUND
pusimos	poniendo
pusisteis	
pusieron	PAST PARTICIPLE
	puesto

Other verbs that follow this model:
anteponer, aponer, componer, contraponer, deponer,
descomponer, disponer, exponer, imponer, indisponer,

interponer, oponer, posponer, predisponer, preponer, presuponer, proponer, recomponer, reponer, sobreexponer, sobreponer, superponer, suponer, transponer, trasponer, yuxtaponer

67. prohibir (to ban)

PRESENT	PRESENT SUBJUNCTIVE
prohíbo	**prohíb**a
prohíbes	**prohíb**as
prohíbe	**prohíb**a
prohibimos	prohibamos
prohibís	prohibáis
prohíben	**prohíb**an

IMPERFECT	IMPERFECT SUBJUNCTIVE
prohibía	prohibiera/prohibiese
prohibías	prohibieras/prohibieses
prohibía	prohibiera/prohibiese
prohibíamos	prohibiéramos/prohibiésemos
prohibíais	prohibierais/prohibieseis
prohibían	prohibieran/prohibiesen

FUTURE	CONDITIONAL
prohibiré	prohibiría
prohibirás	prohibirías
prohibirá	prohibiría
prohibiremos	prohibiríamos
prohibiréis	prohibiríais
prohibirán	prohibirían

PRETERITE	IMPERATIVE
prohibí	**prohíb**e, prohibid
prohibiste	
prohibió	GERUND
prohibimos	prohibiendo
prohibisteis	
prohibieron	PAST PARTICIPLE
	prohibido

Other verbs that follow this medel:
cohibir

68. pudrir (to rot)

PRESENT	PRESENT SUBJUNCTIVE
pudro	pudra
pudres	pudras
pudre	pudra
pudrimos	pudramos
pudrís	pudráis
pudren	pudran

IMPERFECT	IMPERFECT SUBJUNCTIVE
pudría	pudriera/pudriese
pudrías	pudrieras/pudrieses
pudría	pudriera/pudriese
pudríamos	pudriéramos/pudriésemos
pudríais	pudrierais/pudrieseis
pudrían	pudrieran/pudriesen

FUTURE	CONDITIONAL
pudriré	pudriría
pudrirás	pudrirías
pudrirá	pudriría
pudriremos	pudriríamos
pudriréis	pudriríais
pudrirán	pudrirían

PRETERITE	IMPERATIVE
pudrí	pudre, pudrid
pudriste	
pudrió	GERUND
pudrimos	pudriendo
pudristeis	
pudrieron	PAST PARTICIPLE
	podrido

Other verbs that follow this model:
repudrir

69. querer (to want)

PRESENT	PRESENT SUBJUNCTIVE
quiero	**quier**a
quieres	**quier**as
quiere	**quier**a
queremos	queramos
queréis	queráis
quieren	**quier**an

IMPERFECT	IMPERFECT SUBJUNCTIVE
quería	**quis**iera/**quis**iese
querías	**quis**ieras/**quis**ieses
quería	**quis**iera/**quis**iese
queríamos	**quis**iéramos/**quis**iésemos
queríais	**quis**ierais/**quis**ieseis
querían	**quis**ieran/**quis**iesen

FUTURE	CONDITIONAL
querré	**querr**ía
querrás	**querr**ías
querrá	**querr**ía
querremos	**querr**íamos
querréis	**querr**íais
querrán	**querr**ían

PRETERITE	IMPERATIVE
quise	**quier**e, quered
quisiste	
quiso	GERUND
quisimos	queriendo
quisisteis	
quisieron	PAST PARTICIPLE
	querido

Other verbs that follow this model:
bienquerer, malquerer

70. raer (to scrape)

PRESENT
rao, **raigo**, **rayo**
raes
rae
raemos
raéis
raen

PRESENT SUBJUNCTIVE
raiga/**ray**a
raigas/**ray**as
raiga/**ray**a
raigamos/**ray**amos
raigáis/**ray**áis
raigan/**ray**an

IMPERFECT
raía
raías
raía
raíamos
raíais
raían

IMPERFECT SUBJUNCTIVE
rayera/rayese
rayeras/rayeses
rayera/rayese
rayéramos/rayésemos
rayerais/rayeseis
rayeran/rayesen

FUTURE
raeré
raerás
raerá
raeremos
raeréis
raerán

CONDITIONAL
raería
raerías
raería
raeríamos
raeríais
raerían

PRETERITE
raí
ra**íste**
ra**yó**
ra**ímos**
ra**ísteis**
ra**yeron**

IMPERATIVE
rae, raed

GERUND
ra**yendo**

PAST PARTICIPLE
ra**ído**

71. rehacer (to redo)

PRESENT	PRESENT SUBJUNCTIVE
rehago	rehaga
rehaces	rehagas
rehace	rehaga
rehacemos	rehagamos
rehacéis	rehagáis
rehacen	rehagan

IMPERFECT	IMPERFECT SUBJUNCTIVE
rehacía	rehiciera/rehiciese
rehacías	rehicieras/rehicieses
rehacía	rehiciera/rehiciese
rehacíamos	rehiciéramos/rehiciésemos
rehacíais	rehicierais/rehicieseis
rehacían	rehicieran/rehiciesen

FUTURE	CONDITIONAL
reharé	reharía
reharás	reharías
rehará	reharía
reharemos	reharíamos
reharéis	reharíais
reharán	reharían

PRETERITE	IMPERATIVE
rehíce	rehaz, rehaced
rehiciste	
rehízo	GERUND
rehicimos	rehaciendo
rehicisteis	
rehicieron	PAST PARTICIPLE
	rehecho

72. rehuir (to shun, to avoid)

PRESENT
rehúyo
rehúyes
rehúye
rehuimos
rehuís
rehúyen

PRESENT SUBJUNCTIVE
rehúya
rehúyas
rehúya
rehuyamos
rehuyáis
rehúyan

IMPERFECT
rehuía
rehuías
rehuía
rehuíamos
rehuíais
rehuían

IMPERFECT SUBJUNCTIVE
rehuyera/rehuyese
rehuyeras/rehuyeses
rehuyera/rehuyese
rehuyéramos/rehuyésemos
rehuyerais/rehuyeseis
rehuyeran/rehuyesen

FUTURE
rehuiré
rehuirás
rehuirá
rehuiremos
rehuiréis
rehuirán

CONDITIONAL
rehuiría
rehuirías
rehuiría
rehuiríamos
rehuiríais
rehuirían

PRETERITE
rehuí
rehuiste
rehuyó
rehuimos
rehuisteis
rehuyeron

IMPERATIVE
rehúye, rehuid

GERUND
rehuyendo

PAST PARTICIPLE
rehuido

73. reír (to laugh)

PRESENT
río
ríes
ríe
re**ímos**
reís
ríen

PRESENT SUBJUNCTIVE
ría
rías
ría
riamos
riáis/**riais**
rían

IMPERFECT
reía
reías
reía
reíamos
reíais
reían

IMPERFECT SUBJUNCTIVE
riera/**riese**
rieras/**rieses**
riera/**riese**
riéramos/**riésemos**
rierais/**rieseis**
rieran/**riesen**

FUTURE
reiré
reirás
reirá
reiremos
reiréis
reirán

CONDITIONAL
reiría
reirías
reiría
reiríamos
reiríais
reirían

PRETERITE
reí
re**íste**
ri**ó/rio**
re**ímos**
re**ísteis**
rieron

IMPERATIVE
ríe, re**íd**

GERUND
riendo

PAST PARTICIPLE
re**ído**

Other verbs that follow this model:
desleír, engreír, sonreír

74. reñir (to quarrel)

PRESENT	PRESENT SUBJUNCTIVE
riño	**riñ**a
riñes	**riñ**as
riñe	**riñ**a
reñimos	**riñ**amos
reñís	**riñ**áis
riñen	**riñ**an

IMPERFECT	IMPERFECT SUBJUNCTIVE
reñía	**riñera/riñese**
reñías	**riñeras/riñeses**
reñía	**riñera/riñese**
reñíamos	**riñéramos/riñésemos**
reñíais	**riñerais/riñeseis**
reñían	**riñeran/riñesen**

FUTURE	CONDITIONAL
reñiré	reñiría
reñirás	reñirías
reñirá	reñiría
reñiremos	reñiríamos
reñiréis	reñiríais
reñirán	reñirían

PRETERITE	IMPERATIVE
reñí	**riñ**e, reñid
reñiste	
riñó	GERUND
reñimos	**riñendo**
reñisteis	
riñeron	PAST PARTICIPLE
	reñido

Other verbs that follow this model:
ceñir, constreñir, desceñir, desteñir, estreñir, heñir, reteñir, teñir

75. reunir (to gather together)

PRESENT	PRESENT SUBJUNCTIVE
reúno	**reún**a
reúnes	**reún**as
reúne	**reún**a
reunimos	reunamos
reunís	reunáis
reúnen	**reún**an

IMPERFECT	IMPERFECT SUBJUNCTIVE
reunía	reuniera/reuniese
reunías	reunieras/reunieses
reunía	reuniera/reuniese
reuníamos	reuniéramos/reuniésemos
reuníais	reunierais/reunieseis
reunían	reunieran/reuniesen

FUTURE	CONDITIONAL
reuniré	reuniría
reunirás	reunirías
reunirá	reuniría
reuniremos	reuniríamos
reuniréis	reuniríais
reunirán	reunirían

PRETERITE	IMPERATIVE
reuní	**reún**e, reunid
reuniste	
reunió	GERUND
reunimos	reuniendo
reunisteis	
reunieron	PAST PARTICIPLE
	reunido

76. roer (to gnaw)

PRESENT
roo/**roig**o/**roy**o
roes
roe
roemos
roéis
roen

PRESENT SUBJUNCTIVE
roa/**roig**a/**roy**a
roas/**roig**as/**roy**as
roa/**roig**a/**roy**a
roamos/**roig**amos/**roy**amos
roáis/**roig**áis/**roy**áis
roan/**roig**an/**roy**an

IMPERFECT
roía
roías
roía
roíamos
roíais
roían

IMPERFECT SUBJUNCTIVE
royera/royese
royeras/royeses
royera/royese
royéramos/royésemos
royerais/royeseis
royeran/royesen

FUTURE
roeré
roerás
roerá
roeremos
roeréis
roerán

CONDITIONAL
roería
roerías
roería
roeríamos
roeríais
roerían

PRETERITE
roí
roíste
ro**yó**
ro**ímos**
ro**ísteis**
ro**yeron**

IMPERATIVE
roe, roed

GERUND
ro**yendo**

PAST PARTICIPLE
ro**ído**

Other verbs that follow this model:
corroer

77. rogar (to beg, to pray)

PRESENT	PRESENT SUBJUNCTIVE
ruego	**ruegu**e
ruegas	**ruegu**es
ruega	**ruegu**e
rogamos	**rogu**emos
rogáis	**rogu**éis
ruegan	**ruegu**en

IMPERFECT	IMPERFECT SUBJUNCTIVE
rogaba	rogara/rogase
rogabas	rogaras/rogases
rogaba	rogara/rogase
rogábamos	rogáramos/rogásemos
rogabais	rogarais/rogaseis
rogaban	rogaran/rogasen

FUTURE	CONDITIONAL
rogaré	rogaría
rogarás	rogarías
rogará	rogaría
rogaremos	rogaríamos
rogaréis	rogaríais
rogarán	rogarían

PRETERITE	IMPERATIVE
rogué	**rueg**a, rogad
rogaste	
rogó	GERUND
rogamos	rogando
rogasteis	
rogaron	PAST PARTICIPLE
	rogado

Other verbs that follow this model:
colgar, descolgar, holgar

78. romper (to break)

PRESENT	PRESENT SUBJUNCTIVE
rompo	rompa
rompes	rompas
rompe	rompa
rompemos	rompamos
rompéis	rompáis
rompen	rompan

IMPERFECT	IMPERFECT SUBJUNCTIVE
rompía	rompiera/rompiese
rompías	rompieras/rompieses
rompía	rompiera/rompiese
rompíamos	rompiéramos/rompiésemos
rompíais	rompierais/rompieseis
rompían	rompieran/rompiesen

FUTURE	CONDITIONAL
romperé	rompería
romperás	romperías
romperá	rompería
romperemos	romperíamos
romperéis	romperíais
romperán	romperían

PRETERITE	IMPERATIVE
rompí	rompe, romped
rompiste	
rompió	GERUND
rompimos	rompiendo
rompisteis	
rompieron	PAST PARTICIPLE
	roto

79. saber (to know)

PRESENT
sé
sabes
sabe
sabemos
sabéis
saben

PRESENT SUBJUNCTIVE
sepa
sepas
sepa
sepamos
sepáis
sepan

IMPERFECT
sabía
sabías
sabía
sabíamos
sabíais
sabían

IMPERFECT SUBJUNCTIVE
supiera/**sup**iese
supieras/**sup**ieses
supiera/**sup**iese
supiéramos/**sup**iésemos
supierais/**sup**ieseis
supieran/**sup**iesen

FUTURE
sabré
sabrás
sabrá
sabremos
sabréis
sabrán

CONDITIONAL
sabría
sabrías
sabría
sabríamos
sabríais
sabrían

PRETERITE
supe
supiste
supo
supimos
supisteis
supieron

IMPERATIVE
sabe, sabed

GERUND
sabiendo

PAST PARTICIPLE
sabido

Other verbs that follow this model:
resaber

98

80. sacar (to take out)

PRESENT	PRESENT SUBJUNCTIVE
saco	**saque**
sacas	**saques**
saca	**saque**
sacamos	**saquemos**
sacáis	**saquéis**
sacan	**saquen**

IMPERFECT	IMPERFECT SUBJUNCTIVE
sacaba	sacara/sacase
sacabas	sacaras/sacases
sacaba	sacara/sacase
sacábamos	sacáramos/sacásemos
sacabais	sacarais/sacaseis
sacaban	sacaran/sacasen

FUTURE	CONDITIONAL
sacaré	sacaría
sacarás	sacarías
sacará	sacaría
sacaremos	sacaríamos
sacaréis	sacaríais
sacarán	sacarían

PRETERITE	IMPERATIVE
saqué	saca, sacad
sacaste	
sacó	GERUND
sacamos	sacando
sacasteis	
sacaron	PAST PARTICIPLE
	sacado

Other verbs that follow this model:
abanicar, abarcar, abdicar, abellacar, abocar, aborrascarse, abroncar, acercar, achacar, achicar, achocar, acidificar,

acuchucar, acurrucarse, adjudicar, advocar, afincar, ahorcar,
ahuecar, alambicar, altercar, amoscarse, amplificar,
apalancar, apanicar, apañuscar, aparcar, apencar,
apeñuscarse, aplacar, aplicar, apocar, ariscar, arrancar,
arrascar, arriscar, atacar, atascar, atrabancar, atracar, atrancar,
atrincar, autenticar, autentificar, avocar, bancar, beatificar,
becar, bifurcarse, bilocarse, bisecar, blocar, bonificar, brincar,
buscar, caducar, calcar, calcificar, calificar, capiscar, cascar,
centuplicar, cercar, certificar, chamuscar, chancar, chascar,
chocar, churruscar, ciscar, clarificar, clasificar, claudicar,
codificar, cofabricar, colocar, comarcar, comiscar, complicar,
comunicar, conculcar, confiscar, contraatacar, contraindicar,
contrarreplicar, convocar, coscarse, cosificar, criticar,
cronificar, crucificar, cuacar, cuadruplicar, cualificar,
cuantificar, cubicar, cucar, damnificar, debocar, decalcificar,
decodificar, decorticar, dedicar, defecar, deificar, demarcar,
densificar, deprecar, derrocar, desacidificar, desaparcar,
desaplicar, desatancar, desatascar, desatrancar, desbancar,
desbarrancar, desbocar, descalificar, descascar, descercar,
desclasificar, descocarse, descodificar, descolocar,
desconvocar, desecar, desembarcar, desembarrancar,
desembocar, desempacar, desenfocar, desenroscar,
desertificar, desfalcar, deshipotecar, desintoxicar, desmarcar,
desmitificar, desnucar, despelucar, despotricar, destacar,
desubicar, diagnosticar, dignificar, discar, disecar, dislocar,
diversificar, domesticar, dosificar, dulcificar, duplicar,
edificar, educar, ejemplificar, electrificar, embancarse,
embarcar, embarrancar, embaucar, embelecar, embicar,
embocar, emborrascarse, emboscar, embrocar, embroncarse,
empacar, empericarse, enamoricarse, enarcar, encalamocar,
encharcar, enfocar, enfoscar, enfrascarse, enmarcar, enrocar,
enroscar, ensacar, entabicar, entarascar, entrechocar,
entresacar, entroncar, enzocar, equivocar, erradicar,
escarificar, escenificar, esparrancarse, especificar, estancar,
estatificar, estratificar, estucar, estultificar, evocar, explicar,
fabricar, falsificar, fincar, fornicar, fortificar, fructificar,
gasificar, glorificar, gratificar, hamacar, hincar, hipotecar,
hocicar, humidificar, identificar, imbricar, implicar, imprecar,

impurificar, incomunicar, inculcar, indicar, intensificar, intercomunicar, intoxicar, intrincar, invocar, justificar, lacar, lamiscar, lascar, lenificar, lentificar, lignificar, lubricar, lubrificar, macarse, machacar, machucar, magnificar, maleducar, mancar, manducar, marcar, mascar, masificar, masticar, mechificar, medicar, mercar, mistificar, mitificar, mixtificar, modificar, molificar, mordicar, mortificar, multiplicar, musicar, neviscar, nidificar, notificar, obcecar, ofuscar, oliscar, opacar, osificarse, pacificar, panificar, pecar, pellizcar, pencar, perjudicar, personificar, pescar, petrificar, picar, piscar, pizcar, placar, planificar, plantificar, plastificar, platicar, pontificar, practicar, predicar, prefabricar, prevaricar, pronosticar, prosificar, provocar, publicar, purificar, quintuplicar, radicar, ramificarse, rarificar, rascar, ratificar, rebuscar, recalcar, recalificar, reciprocar, recolocar, rectificar, reduplicar, reedificar, reeducar, reembarcar, refrescar, reivindicar, remarcar, remolcar, repescar, repicar, replicar, resecar, retocar, retrancar, retrucar, reubicar, reunificar, revindicar, revivificar, revocar, roncar, rubricar, sacarificar, sacrificar, salificar, salpicar, santificar, saponificar, secar, septuplicar, sextuplicar, significar, simplificar, sindicar, socar, sofisticar, sofocar, solidificar, sonsacar, suberificarse, suplicar, surcar, tabicar, tacar, tapiscar, tarascar, tascar, tecnificar, testificar, tipificar, tocar, tonificar, torrificar, trabucar, traficar, trambucar, trancar, trasbucar, trasbuscar, trincar, triplicar, triscar, trisecar, trompicar, trucar, truncar, ubicar, unificar, vacar, ventiscar, verificar, versificar, vindicar, vitrificar, vivificar, zambucar

81. salir (to go out)

PRESENT	PRESENT SUBJUNCTIVE
salgo	**salg**a
sales	**salg**as
sale	**salg**a
salimos	**salg**amos
salís	**salg**áis
salen	**salg**an

IMPERFECT	IMPERFECT SUBJUNCTIVE
salía	saliera/saliese
salías	salieras/salieses
salía	saliera/saliese
salíamos	saliéramos/saliésemos
salíais	salierais/salieseis
salían	salieran/saliesen

FUTURE	CONDITIONAL
saldré	**saldr**ía
saldrás	**saldr**ías
saldrá	**saldr**ía
saldremos	**saldr**íamos
saldréis	**saldr**íais
saldrán	**saldr**ían

PRETERITE	IMPERATIVE
salí	**sal**, salid
saliste	
salió	GERUND
salimos	saliendo
salisteis	
salieron	PAST PARTICIPLE
	salido

Other verbs that follow this model:
sobresalir

82. seguir (to follow)

PRESENT	PRESENT SUBJUNCTIVE
sigo	**sig**a
sigues	**sig**as
sigue	**sig**a
seguimos	**sig**amos
seguís	**sig**áis
siguen	**sig**an

IMPERFECT	IMPERFECT SUBJUNCTIVE
seguía	**sigu**iera/**sigu**iese
seguías	**sigu**ieras/**sigu**ieses
seguía	**sigu**iera/**sigu**iese
seguíamos	**sigu**iéramos/**sigu**iésemos
seguíais	**sigu**ierais/**sigu**ieseis
seguían	**sigu**ieran/**sigu**iesen

FUTURE	CONDITIONAL
seguiré	seguiría
seguirás	seguirías
seguirá	seguiría
seguiremos	seguiríamos
seguiréis	seguiríais
seguirán	seguirían

PRETERITE	IMPERATIVE
seguí	**sigu**e, seguid
seguiste	
siguió	GERUND
seguimos	**sigu**iendo
seguisteis	
siguieron	PAST PARTICIPLE
	seguido

Other verbs that follow this model:
conseguir, perseguir, proseguir, subseguir

83. sentir (to feel)

PRESENT	PRESENT SUBJUNCTIVE
siento	**sient**a
sientes	**sient**as
siente	**sient**a
sentimos	**sint**amos
sentís	**sint**áis
sienten	**sient**an

IMPERFECT	IMPERFECT SUBJUNCTIVE
sentía	**sint**iera/**sint**iese
sentías	**sint**ieras/**sint**ieses
sentía	**sint**iera/**sint**iese
sentíamos	**sint**iéramos/**sint**iésemos
sentíais	**sint**ierais/**sint**ieseis
sentían	**sint**ieran/**sint**iesen

FUTURE	CONDITIONAL
sentiré	sentiría
sentirás	sentirías
sentirá	sentiría
sentiremos	sentiríamos
sentiréis	sentiríais
sentirán	sentirían

PRETERITE	IMPERATIVE
sentí	**sient**e, sentid
sentiste	
sintió	GERUND
sentimos	**sint**iendo
sentisteis	
sintieron	PAST PARTICIPLE
	sentido

Other verbs that follow this model:
adherir, advertir, arrepentirse, asentir, circunferir, conferir, consentir, controvertir, convertir, deferir, desadvertir,

desinvertir, desmentir, diferir, digerir, disentir, divertir, engerirse, herir, hervir, inferir, ingerir, injerir, interferir, invertir, malherir, mentir, pervertir, preferir, presentir, preterir, proferir, reconvertir, referir, reinvertir, requerir, resentirse, revertir, subvertir, sugerir, transferir, trasferir, zaherir

84. ser (to be)

PRESENT	PRESENT SUBJUNCTIVE
soy	**se**a
eres	**se**as
es	**se**a
somos	**se**amos
sois	**se**áis
son	**se**an

IMPERFECT	IMPERFECT SUBJUNCTIVE
era	**fuera/fuese**
eras	**fueras/fueses**
era	**fuera/fuese**
éramos	**fuéramos/fuésemos**
erais	**fuerais/fueseis**
eran	**fueran/fuesen**

FUTURE	CONDITIONAL
seré	sería
serás	serías
será	sería
seremos	seríamos
seréis	seríais
serán	serían

PRETERITE	IMPERATIVE
fui	s**é**, sed
fuiste	
fue	GERUND
fuimos	siendo
fuisteis	
fueron	PAST PARTICIPLE
	sido

85. tañer (to strum)

PRESENT	PRESENT SUBJUNCTIVE
taño	taña
tañes	tañas
tañe	taña
tañemos	tañamos
tañéis	tañáis
tañen	tañan

IMPERFECT	IMPERFECT SUBJUNCTIVE
tañía	tañera/tañese
tañías	tañeras/tañeses
tañía	tañera/tañese
tañíamos	tañéramos/tañésemos
tañíais	tañerais/tañeseis
tañían	tañeran/tañesen

FUTURE	CONDITIONAL
tañeré	tañería
tañerás	tañerías
tañerá	tañería
tañeremos	tañeríamos
tañeréis	tañeríais
tañerán	tañerían

PRETERITE	IMPERATIVE
tañí	tañe, tañed
tañiste	
tañó	GERUND
tañimos	tañendo
tañisteis	
tañeron	PAST PARTICIPLE
	tañido

Other verbs that follow this model:
atañer

86. tener (to have)

PRESENT	PRESENT SUBJUNCTIVE
tengo	**teng**a
tienes	**teng**as
tiene	**teng**a
tenemos	**teng**amos
tenéis	**teng**áis
tienen	**teng**an

IMPERFECT	IMPERFECT SUBJUNCTIVE
tenía	**tuv**iera/**tuv**iese
tenías	**tuv**ieras/**tuv**ieses
tenía	**tuv**iera/**tuv**iese
teníamos	**tuv**iéramos/**tuv**iésemos
teníais	**tuv**ierais/**tuv**ieseis
tenían	**tuv**ieran/**tuv**iesen

FUTURE	CONDITIONAL
tendré	**tendr**ía
tendrás	**tendr**ías
tendrá	**tendr**ía
tendremos	**tendr**íamos
tendréis	**tendr**íais
tendrán	**tendr**ían

PRETERITE	IMPERATIVE
tuve	**ten**, tened
tuviste	
tuvo	GERUND
tuvimos	teniendo
tuvisteis	
tuvieron	PAST PARTICIPLE
	tenido

Other verbs that follow this model:
abstenerse, atenerse, autosostenerse, contener, detener,
entretener, mantener, manutener, obtener, retener, sostener

87. traer (to bring)

PRESENT	PRESENT SUBJUNCTIVE
traigo	**traig**a
traes	**traig**as
trae	**traig**a
traemos	**traig**amos
traéis	**traig**áis
traen	**traig**an

IMPERFECT	IMPERFECT SUBJUNCTIVE
traía	**trajera/trajese**
traías	**trajeras/trajeses**
traía	**trajera/trajese**
traíamos	**trajéramos/trajésemos**
traíais	**trajerais/trajeseis**
traían	**trajeran/trajesen**

FUTURE	CONDITIONAL
traeré	traería
traerás	traerías
traerá	traería
traeremos	traeríamos
traeréis	traeríais
traerán	traerían

PRETERITE	IMPERATIVE
traje	trae, traed
trajiste	
trajo	GERUND
trajimos	tra**yendo**
trajisteis	
trajeron	PAST PARTICIPLE
	tra**í**do

Other verbs that follow this model:
abstraer, atraer, contraer, detraer, distraer, extraer, maltraer, retraer, retrotraer, substraer, sustraer

88. valer (to be worth)

PRESENT	PRESENT SUBJUNCTIVE
valgo	**valg**a
vales	**valg**as
vale	**valg**a
valemos	**valg**amos
valéis	**valg**áis
valen	**valg**an

IMPERFECT	IMPERFECT SUBJUNCTIVE
valía	valiera/valiese
valías	valieras/valieses
valía	valiera/valiese
valíamos	valiéramos/valiésemos
valíais	valierais/valieseis
valían	valieran/valiesen

FUTURE	CONDITIONAL
valdré	**valdr**ía
valdrás	**valdr**ías
valdrá	**valdr**ía
valdremos	**valdr**íamos
valdréis	**valdr**íais
valdrán	**valdr**ían

PRETERITE	IMPERATIVE
valí	vale, valed
valiste	
valió	GERUND
valimos	valiendo
valisteis	
valieron	PAST PARTICIPLE
	valido

Other verbs that follow this model:
equivaler, prevalerse

89. vencer (to defeat)

PRESENT	PRESENT SUBJUNCTIVE
venzo	**venz**a
vences	**venz**as
vence	**venz**a
vencemos	**venz**amos
vencéis	**venz**áis
vencen	**venz**an

IMPERFECT	IMPERFECT SUBJUNCTIVE
vencía	venciera/venciese
vencías	vencieras/vencieses
vencía	venciera/venciese
vencíamos	venciéramos/venciésemos
vencíais	vencierais/vencieseis
vencían	vencieran/venciesen

FUTURE	CONDITIONAL
venceré	vencería
vercerás	vencerías
vercerá	vencería
verceremos	venceríamos
verceréis	venceríais
vercerán	vencerían

PRETERITE	IMPERATIVE
vencí	vence, venced
venciste	
venció	GERUND
vencimos	venciendo
vencisteis	
vencieron	PAST PARTICIPLE
	vencido

Other verbs that follow this model:
coercer, convencer, ejercer, mecer, remecer

90. venir (to come)

PRESENT	PRESENT SUBJUNCTIVE
vengo	**veng**a
vienes	**veng**as
viene	**veng**a
venimos	**veng**amos
venís	**veng**áis
vienen	**veng**an

IMPERFECT	IMPERFECT SUBJUNCTIVE
venía	**vin**iera/**vin**iese
venías	**vin**ieras/**vin**ieses
venía	**vin**iera/**vin**iese
veníamos	**vin**iéramos/**vin**iésemos
veníais	**vin**ierais/**vin**ieseis
venían	**vin**ieran/**vin**iesen

FUTURE	CONDITIONAL
vendré	**vendr**ía
vendrás	**vendr**ías
vendrá	**vendr**ía
vendremos	**vendr**íamos
vendréis	**vendr**íais
vendrán	**vendr**ían

PRETERITE	IMPERATIVE
vine	**ven**, venid
viniste	
vino	GERUND
vinimos	**vin**iendo
vinisteis	
vinieron	PAST PARTICIPLE
	venido

Other verbs that follow this model:

advenir, avenir, contravenir, convenir, desavenir, desconvenir, devenir, intervenir, prevenir, provenir, reconvenir, revenirse, sobrevenir, subvenir

91. ver (to see)

PRESENT	PRESENT SUBJUNCTIVE
veo	**ve**a
ves	**ve**as
ve	**ve**a
vemos	**ve**amos
v**eis**	**ve**áis
ven	**ve**an

IMPERFECT	IMPERFECT SUBJUNCTIVE
veía	viera/viese
veías	vieras/vieses
veía	viera/viese
veíamos	viéramos/viésemos
veíais	vierais/vieseis
veían	vieran/viesen

FUTURE	CONDITIONAL
veré	vería
verás	verías
verá	vería
veremos	veríamos
veréis	veríais
verán	verían

PRETERITE	IMPERATIVE
v**i**	ve, ved
viste	
v**io**	GERUND
vimos	viendo
visteis	
vieron	PAST PARTICIPLE
	visto

Other verbs that follow this model:
entrever, prever, rever

92. volcar (to overturn)

PRESENT	PRESENT SUBJUNCTIVE
vuelco	**vuelqu**e
vuelcas	**vuelqu**es
vuelca	**vuelqu**e
volcamos	**volqu**emos
volcáis	**volqu**éis
vuelcan	**vuelqu**en

IMPERFECT	IMPERFECT SUBJUNCTIVE
volcaba	volcara/volcase
volcabas	volcaras/volcases
volcaba	volcara/volcase
volcábamos	volcáramos/volcásemos
volcabais	volcarais/volcaseis
volcaban	volcaran/volcasen

FUTURE	CONDITIONAL
volcaré	volcaría
volcarás	volcarías
volcará	volcaría
volcaremos	volcaríamos
volcaréis	volcaríais
volcarán	volcarían

PRETERITE	IMPERATIVE
volqué	**vuelc**a, volcad
volcaste	
volcó	GERUND
volcamos	volcando
volcasteis	
volcaron	PAST PARTICIPLE
	volcado

Other verbs that follow this model:
aporcar, emporcar, revolcar, trastocar, trastrocar, trocar

93. volver (to return)

PRESENT	PRESENT SUBJUNCTIVE
vuelvo	**vuelv**a
vuelves	**vuelv**as
vuelve	**vuelv**a
volvemos	volvamos
volvéis	volváis
vuelven	**vuelv**an

IMPERFECT	IMPERFECT SUBJUNCTIVE
volvía	volviera/volviese
volvías	volvieras/volvieses
volvía	volviera/volviese
volvíamos	volviéramos/volviésemos
volvíais	volvierais/volvieseis
volvían	volvieran/volviesen

FUTURE	CONDITIONAL
volveré	volvería
volverás	volverías
volverá	volvería
volveremos	volveríamos
volveréis	volveríais
volverán	volverían

PRETERITE	IMPERATIVE
volví	**vuelv**e, volved
volviste	
volvió	GERUND
volvimos	volviendo
volvisteis	
volvieron	PAST PARTICIPLE
	vuelto

Other verbs that follow this model:
absolver, desenvolver, devolver, desvolver, disolver, ensolver, envolver, resolver, revolver

94. yacer (to lie)

PRESENT
yazco/**yazg**o/**yag**o
yaces
yace
yacemos
yacéis
yacen

PRESENT SUBJUNCTIVE
yazca/**yazg**a/**yag**a
yazcas/**yazg**as/**yag**as
yazca/**yazg**a/**yag**a
yazcamos/**yazg**amos/**yag**amos
yazcáis/**yazg**áis/**yag**áis
yazcan/**yazg**an/**yag**an

IMPERFECT
yacía
yacías
yacía
yacíamos
yacíais
yacían

IMPERFECT SUBJUNCTIVE
yaciera/yaciese
yacieras/yacieses
yaciera/yaciese
yaciéramos/yaciésemos
yacierais/yacieseis
yacieran/yaciesen

FUTURE
yaceré
yacerás
yacerá
yaceremos
yaceréis
yacerán

CONDITIONAL
yacería
yacerías
yacería
yaceríamos
yaceríais
yacerían

PRETERITE
yací
yaciste
yació
yacimos
yacisteis
yacieron

IMPERATIVE
yace/**yaz**, yaced

GERUND
yaciendo

PAST PARTICIPLE
yacido

Other verbs that follow this model:
subyacer

95. zurcir (to darn)

PRESENT	PRESENT SUBJUNCTIVE
zurzo	**zurz**a
zurces	**zurz**as
zurce	**zurz**a
zurcimos	**zurz**amos
zurcís	**zurz**áis
zurcen	**zurz**an

IMPERFECT	IMPERFECT SUBJUNCTIVE
zurcía	zurciera/zurciese
zurcías	zurcieras/zurcieses
zurcía	zurciera/zurciese
zurcíamos	zurciéramos/zurciésemos
zurcíais	zurcierais/zurcieseis
zurcían	zurcieran/zurciesen

FUTURE	CONDITIONAL
zurciré	zurciría
zurcirás	zurcirías
zurcirá	zurciría
zurciremos	zurciríamos
zurciréis	zurciríais
zurcirán	zurcirían

PRETERITE	IMPERATIVE
zurcí	zurce, zurcid
zurciste	
zurció	GERUND
zurcimos	zurciendo
zurcisteis	
zurcieron	PAST PARTICIPLE
	zurcido

Other verbs that follow this model:
desuncir, esparcir, estarcir, fruncir, resarcir, uncir

Verb Index

acribillar (1)
acriollarse (1)
activar (1)
actualizar (26)
actuar (6)
acuatizar (26)
acuchucar (80)
acuciar (1)
acuclillarse (1)
acudir (3)
acumular (1)
acuñar (1)
acurrucarse (80)
acusar (1)
adaptar (1)
adecuar (1)
adelantar (1)
adelgazar (26)
adentrarse (1)
aderezar (26)
adeudar (1)
adherir (83)
adicionar (1)
adiestrar (1)
adivinar (1)
adjudicar (80)
adjuntar (1)
administrar (1)
admirar (1)
admitir (3)
adocenarse (1)
adoctrinar (1)
adolecer (25)
adoptar (1)
adorar (1)
adormecer (25)
adormilarse (1)
adornar (1)

adosar (1)
adquirir (7)
adscribir (44)
aducir (22)
adueñarse (1)
adular (1)
adulterar (1)
advenir (90)
adverbializar (26)
advertir (83)
advocar (80)
aeroenviar (41)
afamar (1)
afanarse (1)
afear (1)
afeccionarse (1)
afectar (1)
afeitar (1)
aferrar (1)
afianzar (26)
aficionar (1)
afilar (1)
afiliarse (1)
afinar (1)
afincar (80)
afirmar (1)
afligir (32)
aflojar (1)
afluir (23)
afollarse (24)
aforar (24)
afrentar (1)
africanizar (26)
afrontar (1)
agachar (1)
agarrar (1)
agarrotar (1)

agasajar (1)
agilizar (26)
agitar (1)
aglomerarse (1)
agobiar (1)
agolparse (1)
agonizar (26)
agotar (1)
agraciar (1)
agradar (1)
agradecer (25)
agrandar (1)
agravar (1)
agraviar (1)
agrazar (26)
agredir (4)
agregar (61)
agriar (1)
agrietarse (1)
agringarse (61)
agrupar (1)
aguantar (1)
aguar (16)
aguardar (1)
aguazar (26)
agudizar (26)
aguerrir (4)
aguijar (1)
aguijonear (1)
agujerear (1)
aguzar (26)
ahijar (9)
ahilar (9)
ahincar (8)
ahitar (9)
ahogar (61)
ahondar (1)
ahorcar (80)

ahorrar (1)
ahuecar (80)
ahumar (14)
ahusar (14)
ahuyentar (1)
airar (9)
airear (1)
aislar (9)
ajar (1)
ajustar (1)
ajusticiar (1)
alabar (1)
alabear (1)
alagarse (61)
alambicar (80)
alamparse (1)
alardear (1)
alargar (61)
albergar (61)
alborotar (1)
alborozar (26)
alcalinizar (26)
alcanzar (26)
alcoholizar (26)
aleatorizar (26)
aleccionar (1)
alechugar (61)
alegar (61)
alegorizar (26)
alegrar (1)
alejar (1)
alentar (63)
aletargar (61)
aletear (1)
alfabetizar (26)
alfombrar (1)
aliar (41)
aligerar (1)

alimentar (1)
aliñar (1)
alinear (1)
alisar (1)
alistar (1)
aliviar (1)
allanar (1)
allegar (61)
almacenar (1)
almidonar (1)
almohazar (26)
almorzar (10)
alojar (1)
alquilar (1)
alterar (1)
altercar (80)
alternar (1)
alucinar (1)
aludir (3)
alumbrar (1)
alunizar (26)
aluzar (26)
alzar (26)
amadrigar (61)
amaestrar (1)
amagar (61)
amainar (1)
amalgamar (1)
amamantar (1)
amanecer (25)
amanerarse (1)
amansar (1)
amar (1)
amargar (61)
amarizar (26)
amarrar (1)
amartillar (1)
ambicionar (1)

amedrentar (1)
amenazar (26)
amenguar (16)
amenizar (26)
americanizar (26)
amerizar (26)
amigar (61)
amilanar (1)
aminorar (1)
amistar (1)
amnistiar (41)
amoblar (24)
amodorrarse (1)
amohinar (9)
amolar (24)
amoldar (1)
amonestar (1)
amontonar (1)
amordazar (26)
amortajar (1)
amortiguar (16)
amortizar (26)
amoscarse (80)
amostazar (26)
amotinar (1)
amparar (1)
ampliar (41)
amplificar (80)
amputar (1)
amueblar (1)
amurallar (1)
amusgar (61)
añadir (3)
analizar (26)
anarquizar (26)
anatematizar (26)

Verb Index

anatomizar (26)
anclar (1)
andar (11)
anegar (61)
anexar (1)
anexionar (1)
angustiar (1)
anhelar (1)
anidar (1)
animalizar (26)
animar (1)
aniquilar (1)
anochecer (25)
anonadar (1)
anotar (1)
anquilosarse (1)
ansiar (41)
anteceder (2)
antecoger (21)
antepagar (61)
anteponer (66)
anticipar (1)
antipatizar (26)
antojarse (1)
anudar (1)
anular (1)
anunciar (1)
añejar (1)
aovar (1)
aovillarse (1)
apabullar (1)
apacentar (63)
apaciguar (16)
apadrinar (1)
apagar (61)
apalabrar (1)
apalancar (80)
apalear (1)

apanicar (80)
apañar (1)
apañuscar (80)
aparcar (80)
aparecer (25)
aparejar (1)
aparentar (1)
aparragarse (61)
apartar (1)
apasionarse (1)
apearse (1)
apechugar (61)
apedrear (1)
apegarse (61)
apelar (1)
apellidar (1)
apelmazar (26)
apelotonarse (1)
apenar (1)
apencar (80)
apeñuscarse (80)
apeorar (1)
apercibir (3)
apersogar (61)
apersonarse (1)
apesadumbrar (1)
apesgar (61)
apestar (1)
apetecer (25)
apiadarse (1)
apilar (1)
apiñarse (1)
aplacar (80)
aplanar (1)
aplastar (1)
aplaudir (3)
aplazar (26)

aplicar (80)
apocar (80)
apodar (1)
apoderar (1)
aponer (66)
aporcar (92)
aporrar (1)
aporrear (1)
aportar (1)
aposentarse (1)
apostar (24)
apoyar (1)
apreciar (1)
aprehender (2)
apremiar (1)
aprender (2)
aprensar (1)
apresar (1)
aprestarse (1)
apresurarse (1)
apretar (63)
aprisionar (1)
aprobar (24)
apropiar (1)
aprovechar (1)
aproximar (1)
apuñalar (1)
apuntalar (1)
apuntar (1)
apurar (1)
aquejar (1)
aquietar (1)
arabizar (26)
arañar (1)
arar (1)
arbitrar (1)
arbolar (1)
arcaizar (39)

archivar (1)
arder (2)
arengar (61)
argamasar (1)
argüir (12)
argumentar (1)
ariscar (80)
armar (1)
armonizar (26)
aromatizar (26)
arquear (1)
arraigar (61)
arrancar (80)
arrasar (1)
arrascar (80)
arrastrar (1)
arrear (1)
arrebatar (1)
arrebozar (26)
arrecirse (4)
arredrar (1)
arregazar (26)
arreglar (1)
arremangar (61)
arremeter (2)
arrendar (63)
arrepanchigarse (61)
arrepentirse (83)
arrestar (1)
arriar (41)
arribar (1)
arriesgar (61)
arrimar (1)
arrinconar (1)
arriscar (80)
arrizar (26)
arrodillarse (1)

arrogar (61)
arrojar (1)
arropar (1)
arrostrar (1)
arrugar (61)
arruinar (1)
arrullar (1)
articular (1)
artificializar (26)
asaltar (1)
asar (1)
ascender (40)
asear (1)
asediar (1)
asegurar (1)
asemejarse (1)
asentar (63)
asentir (83)
aserrar (63)
asesinar (1)
aseverar (1)
asfixiar (1)
asignar (1)
asimilar (1)
asir (13)
asistir (3)
asociar (1)
asolar (24)
asolear (1)
asomar (1)
asombrar (1)
asonar (24)
aspar (1)
asperger (21)
aspirar (1)
asquear (1)
astringir (32)
asumir (3)

asustar (1)
atacar (80)
atafagar (61)
atañer (85)
atar (1)
atardecer (25)
atarear (1)
atarragarse (61)
atarugar (61)
atascar (80)
ataviar (41)
atemorizar (26)
atemperar (1)
atenazar (26)
atender (40)
atenerse (86)
atentar (1)
atenuar (6)
aterirse (4)
aterrar (63)
aterrizar (26)
aterrorizar (26)
atesorar (1)
atestar (63)
atestiguar (16)
atezar (26)
atiborrar (1)
atildar (1)
atingir (32)
atisbar (1)
atizar (26)
atollar (1)
atomizar (26)
atontar (1)
atorar (1)
atormentar (1)
atornillar (1)
atosigar (61)

colmar (1)
colocar (80)
colonizar (26)
colorear (1)
colorir (3)
columbrar (1)
columpiar (1)
comadrear (1)
comandar (1)
comarcar (80)
combar (1)
combatir (3)
combinar (1)
comedirse (62)
comentar (1)
comenzar (38)
comer (2)
comercializar (26)
comerciar (1)
cometer (2)
comiscar (80)
comisionar (1)
compactar (1)
compadecer (25)
comparar (1)
comparecer (25)
compartir (3)
compatibilizar (26)
compeler (2)
compendiar (1)
compensar (1)
competer (2)
competir (62)
compilar (1)
complacer (64)
completar (1)

complicar (80)
componer (66)
comportarse (1)
comprar (1)
comprender (2)
comprimir (3)
comprobar (24)
comprometer (2)
compungir (32)
computadorizar (26)
computar (1)
computarizar (26)
computerizar (26)
comulgar (61)
comunicar (80)
comunizar (26)
concatenar (1)
concebir (62)
conceder (2)
concentrar (1)
conceptualizar (26)
conceptuar (6)
concernir (33)
concertar (63)
concienciar (1)
conciliar (1)
concluir (23)
concordar (24)
concretar (1)
concretizar (26)
conculcar (80)
concurrir (3)
condecorar (1)
condenar (1)

condensar (1)
condescender (40)
condolerse (56)
conducir (22)
conectar (1)
confeccionar (1)
conferir (83)
confesar (63)
confiar (41)
configurar (1)
confinar (1)
confirmar (1)
confiscar (80)
confluir (23)
conformar (1)
confortar (1)
confraternizar (26)
confrontar (1)
confundir (3)
congelar (1)
congeniar (1)
congratular (1)
congregar (61)
conjeturar (1)
conjugar (61)
conllevar (1)
conmemorar (1)
conminar (1)
conmover (56)
connaturalizarse (26)
conocer (25)
conquistar (1)
consagrar (1)
conseguir (82)
consensuar (6)

desconceptuar (6)
desconcertar (63)
desconectar (1)
desconfiar (41)
desconocer (25)
desconsolar (24)
descontar (24)
descontextualizar (26)
desconvenir (90)
desconvocar (80)
descorazonar (1)
descorchar (1)
descornar (24)
descorrer (2)
descortezar (26)
descoser (2)
descoyuntar (1)
descreer (53)
describir (44)
descruzar (26)
descuajar (1)
descuajaringar (61)
descuajeringar (61)
descuartizar (26)
descubrir (5)
descuidar (1)
desculpabilizar (26)
desdecir (28)
desdeñar (1)
desdinerar (1)
desdoblar (1)

desdramatizar (26)
desear (1)
desecar (80)
desechar (1)
desegregar (61)
desembalar (1)
desembarazar (26)
desembarcar (80)
desembargar (61)
desembarrancar (80)
desembocar (80)
desembragar (61)
desembriagar (61)
desempacar (80)
desempeñar (1)
desencadenar (1)
desencajar (1)
desencoger (21)
desencontrarse (24)
desenfocar (80)
desengañar (1)
desenlazar (26)
desenmarañar (1)
desenredar (1)
desenroscar (80)
desentenderse (40)
desenterrar (63)
desentrañar (1)

desentronizar (26)
desentumecer (25)
desenvolver (93)
desertar (1)
desertificar (80)
desertizar (26)
desesperanzar (26)
desesperar (1)
desestabilizar (26)
desestimar (1)
desfalcar (80)
desfallecer (25)
desfavorecer (25)
desfigurar (1)
desfilar (1)
desfiscalizar (26)
desfogar (61)
desforestar (1)
desgajar (1)
desgañitarse (1)
desgarrar (1)
desgastar (1)
desgobernar (63)
desgoznar (1)
desgravar (1)
desguañangar (61)
desguarnecer (25)
desguazar (26)
deshabituar (6)
deshacer (49)
deshechizar (26)

Verb Index

deshelar (63)
desherbar (63)
desheredar (1)
deshilar (1)
deshilvanar (1)
deshinchar (1)
deshipotecar (80)
deshonrar (1)
deshumanizar (26)
designar (1)
desilusionar (1)
desincentivar (1)
desindustrializar (26)
desinfectar (1)
desinflar (1)
desinhibir (3)
desintoxicar (80)
desinvertir (83)
desistir (3)
deslegalizar (26)
desleír (73)
deslenguarse (16)
desliar (41)
desligar (61)
deslizar (26)
deslucir (54)
deslumbrar (1)
desmandarse (1)
desmantelar (1)
desmarcar (80)
desmayar (1)
desmedirse (62)
desmejorar (1)
desmembrar (63)

desmentir (83)
desmenuzar (26)
desmerecer (25)
desmigajar (1)
desmigar (61)
desmilitarizar (26)
desmineralizarse (26)
desmitificar (80)
desmonetizar (26)
desmontar (1)
desmoralizar (26)
desmoronarse (1)
desmovilizar (26)
desnacionalizar (26)
desnarigar (61)
desnaturalizar (26)
desnucar (80)
desnudar (1)
desobedecer (25)
desobstruir (23)
desocupar (1)
desodorizar (26)
desoír (59)
desolar (24)
desolidarizarse (26)
desollar (24)
desorganizar (26)
desorientar (1)

desosar (31)
desovar (1)
despabilar (1)
despachar (1)
desparramar (1)
despatriar (1)
despechugarse (61)
despedazar (26)
despedir (62)
despegar (61)
despejar (1)
despelucar (80)
despenalizar (26)
despercudir (3)
desperdigar (61)
desperezarse (26)
despersonalizar (26)
despertar (63)
despiezar (26)
despintar (1)
despistar (1)
desplacer (64)
desplazar (26)
desplegar (58)
despoblar (24)
despojar (1)
despolitizar (26)
desporrondingarse (61)
desposeer (53)
despotizar (26)
despotricar (80)
despreciar (1)
desprender (2)

despreocuparse (1)
desproteger (21)
desproveer (53)
desratizar (26)
desregular (26)
desrizar (26)
destacar (80)
destapar (1)
destazar (26)
destejer (2)
desteñir (74)
desterrar (63)
destilar (1)
destinar (1)
destituir (23)
destorcer (20)
destornillar (1)
destrabar (1)
destrenzar (26)
destrozar (26)
destruir (23)
desubicar (80)
desuncir (95)
desunir (3)
desvaír (23)
desvalorizar (26)
desvanecer (25)
desvariar (41)
desvelar (1)
desvergonzarse (15)
desvestir (62)
desviar (41)
desvirgar (61)
desvirtuar (6)
desvitalizar (26)
desvivirse (3)

desvolver (93)
detallar (1)
detener (86)
detentar (1)
deterger (21)
deteriorar (1)
determinar (1)
detestar (1)
detonar (1)
devaluar (6)
devastar (1)
devengar (61)
devenir (90)
devolver (93)
devorar (1)
diagnosticar (80)
dialogar (61)
dibujar (1)
dictar (1)
diferenciar (1)
diferir (83)
dificultar (1)
difuminar (1)
difundir (3)
digerir (83)
digitalizar (26)
dignarse (1)
dignificar (80)
dilatar (1)
dilucidar (1)
diluir (23)
diluviar (1)
dimitir (3)
dinamizar (26)
diptongar (61)
direccionar (1)
dirigir (32)
dirimir (3)

discar (80)
discernir (33)
disciplinar (1)
discordar (24)
discrepar (1)
disculpar (1)
discurrir (3)
discutir (3)
disecar (80)
diseminar (1)
disentir (83)
disertar (1)
disfrazar (26)
disfrutar (1)
disgregar (61)
disgustar (1)
disimular (1)
disidir (3)
disipar (1)
dislocar (80)
disminuir (23)
disolver (93)
disonar (24)
disparar (1)
dispensar (1)
dispersar (1)
disponer (66)
disputar (1)
distanciar (1)
distar (1)
distender (40)
distinguir (34)
distraer (87)
distribuir (23)
disuadir (3)
divagar (61)
divergir (32)
diversificar (80)

Verb Index

divertir (83)
dividir (3)
divinizar (26)
divorciarse (1)
divulgar (61)
doblar (1)
doblegar (61)
documentar (1)
dogmatizar (26)
doler (56)
domar (1)
domesticar (80)
dominar (1)
donar (1)
dormir (35)
dormitar (1)
dosificar (80)
dotar (1)
dragar (61)
dramatizar (26)
drogar (61)
ducharse (1)
dulcificar (80)
duplicar (80)
durar (1)
echar (1)
ecologizar (26)
economizar (26)
ecualizar (26)
edificar (80)
editar (1)
editorializar (26)
educar (80)
efectuar (6)
efluir (23)
ejecutar (1)
ejemplarizar (26)
ejemplificar (80)

ejercer (89)
elaborar (1)
electrificar (80)
electrizar (26)
electrocutar (1)
elegir (36)
elevar (1)
elidir (3)
eliminar (1)
elogiar (1)
eludir (3)
emanar (1)
emancipar (1)
embadurnar (1)
embaír (37)
embalar (1)
embancarse (80)
embarazar (26)
embarcar (80)
embargar (61)
embarnizar (26)
embarrancar (80)
embarrar (1)
embastecer (25)
embaucar (80)
embaular (14)
embazar (26)
embebecer (25)
embeber (2)
embelecar (80)
embellecer (25)
embestir (62)
embicar (80)
embobar (1)
embocar (80)
embolsar (1)
emborrachar (1)

emborrascarse (80)
emboscar (80)
embotar (1)
embotellar (1)
embotijar (1)
embozar (26)
embragar (61)
embravecer (25)
embriagar (61)
embridar (1)
embrocar (80)
embrollar (1)
embromar (1)
embroncarse (80)
embrutecer (25)
embutir (3)
emerger (21)
emigrar (1)
emitir (3)
emocionar (1)
empacar (80)
empachar (1)
empalagar (61)
empalidecer (25)
empalmar (1)
empañar (1)
empantanarse (1)
empapar (1)
empapelar (1)
empapuzar (26)
empaquetar (1)
emparar (1)
emparedar (1)
emparentar (63)
empastar (1)
empatar (1)

empedernir (4)
empedrar (63)
empellar (1)
empeñar (1)
empeorar (1)
empequeñecer (25)
empericarse (80)
emperrarse (1)
empezar (38)
empinar (1)
emplastecer (25)
emplazar (26)
emplear (1)
empobrecer (25)
empollar (1)
emporcar (92)
empotrar (1)
emprender (2)
empreñar (1)
empujar (1)
empuñar (1)
emular (1)
enaguazar (26)
enajenar (1)
enaltecer (25)
enamorar (1)
enamoricarse (80)
enarcar (80)
enardecer (25)
encabalgar (61)
encabezar (26)
encadenar (1)
encajar (1)
encajonar (1)
encalamocar (80)

encallecer (25)
encamar (1)
encaminar (1)
encandilar (1)
encanecer (25)
encantar (1)
encaramarse (1)
encarcelar (1)
encarecer (25)
encargar (61)
encarnizar (26)
encarrilar (1)
encausar (1)
encauzar (26)
enceguecer (25)
encelar (1)
encenagarse (61)
encender (40)
encentar (63)
encerrar (63)
encharcar (80)
enchufar (1)
enclavar (1)
encoger (21)
encolar (1)
encolerizar (26)
encomendar (63)
encomiar (1)
enconar (1)
encontrar (24)
encorar (24)
encordar (24)
encorvar (1)
encrespar (1)
encuadrar (1)
encubrir (5)
encumbrar (1)
encurtir (3)

endentar (63)
enderezar (26)
endeudarse (1)
endilgar (61)
endomingarse (61)
endosar (1)
endrogarse (61)
endulzar (26)
endurecer (25)
enemistar (1)
energizar (26)
enfadar (1)
enfangar (61)
enfatizar (26)
enfermar (1)
enfervorizar (26)
enflaquecer (25)
enfocar (80)
enfoscar (80)
enfrascarse (80)
enfrentar (1)
enfriar (41)
enfundar (1)
enfurecer(25)
engalanar (1)
engalgar (61)
engañar (1)
enganchar (1)
engarzar (26)
engatusar (1)
engendrar (1)
engerirse (83)
engolfarse (1)
engomar (1)
engordar (1)
engorrar (1)
engranar (1)

engrandecer (25)
engrasar (1)
engreír (73)
engrosar (24)
engrupir (3)
enguarrar (1)
engullir (47)
enhebrar (1)
enhestar (63)
enjabonar (1)
enjaezar (26)
enjalbegar (61)
enjaretar (1)
enjaular (1)
enjuagar (61)
enjugar (61)
enjuiciar (1)
enlatar (1)
enlazar (26)
enlodar (1)
enlodazar (26)
enloquecer (25)
enlucir (54)
enlutar (1)
enmarañar (1)
enmarcar (80)
enmascarar (1)
enmelar (63)
enmendar (63)
enmohecer (25)
enmudecer (25)
ennegrecer (25)
ennoblecer (25)
enojar (1)
enorgullecer (25)
empilchar (1)
enraizar (39)
enrarecer (25)

enrazar (26)
enredar (1)
enriquecer (25)
enrizar (26)
enrocar (80)
enrojecer (25)
enrollar (1)
enronquecer (25)
enroscar (80)
ensacar (80)
ensalzar (26)
ensamblar (1)
ensañarse (1)
ensanchar (1)
ensangrentar (63)
ensartar (1)
ensayar (1)
enseñar (1)
ensillar (1)
ensimismarse (1)
ensoberbecer (25)
ensolver (93)
ensombrecer (25)
ensordecer (25)
ensortijar (1)
ensuciar (1)
entabicar (80)
entablar (1)
entalegar (61)
entallar (1)
entallecer (25)
entapizar (26)
entarascar (80)
entender (40)
enterarse (1)

enternecer (25)
enterrar (63)
entesar (63)
entibiar (1)
entierrar (63)
entonar (1)
entongar (61)
entontecer (25)
entornar (1)
entorpecer (25)
entrar (1)
entreabrir (5)
entrecerrar (63)
entrechocar (80)
entrecoger (21)
entrecruzar (26)
entregar (61)
entrelazar (26)
entrelucir (54)
entremeter (2)
entremezclar (1)
entrenarse (1)
entreoír (59)
entresacar (80)
entretejer (2)
entretener (86)
entrever (91)
entreverar (1)
entrevistar (1)
entristecer (25)
entrometerse (2)
entroncar (80)
entronizar (26)
entullecer (25)
entumecer (25)
enturbiar (1)
entusiasmar (1)
enumerar (1)

enunciar (1)
envainar (1)
envalentonar (1)
envanecer (25)
envasar (1)
envejecer (25)
envenenar (1)
enviar (41)
enviciar (1)
envidiar (1)
envilecer (25)
enviudar (1)
envolver (93)
enyugar (61)
enzarzar (26)
enzocar (80)
equilibrar (1)
equipar (1)
equivaler (88)
equivocar (80)
erguir (42)
erigir (32)
erizar (26)
erogar (61)
erotizar (26)
erradicar (80)
errar (43)
eructar (1)
esbozar (26)
escabullirse (47)
escalar (1)
escaldar (1)
escalofriar (41)
escamar (1)
escampar (1)
escandalizar (26)
escapar (1)
escarbar (1)

escarificar (80)
escarmentar (63)
escarnecer (25)
escasear (1)
escatimar (1)
escenificar (80)
escindir (3)
esclarecer (25)
esclavizar (26)
escocer (20)
escoger (21)
escolarizar (26)
escoltar (1)
escombrar (1)
esconder (2)
escornar (24)
escribir (44)
escrupulizar (26)
escrutar (1)
escuchar (1)
escudarse (1)
escudriñar (1)
esculpir (3)
escupir (3)
escurrir (3)
esforzar (10)
esfumarse (1)
esgrimir (3)
esguazar (26)
eslabonar (1)
esmaltar (1)
esmerarse (1)
espabilar (1)
espaciar (1)
españolizar (26)
espantar (1)
esparcir (95)

esparrancarse
(80)
especializar (26)
especificar (80)
especular (1)
esperanzar (26)
esperar (1)
espesar (1)
espetar (1)
espiar (41)
espigar (61)
espirar (1)
espiritualizar
(26)
espolear (1)
espolvorear (1)
esponjarse (1)
esponsorizar
(26)
esposar (1)
espulgar (61)
esquematizar
(26)
esquiar (41)
esquilar (1)
esquilmar (1)
esquivar (1)
estabilizar (26)
establecer (25)
estacionar (1)
estafar (1)
estallar (1)
estampar (1)
estancar (80)
estandarizar (26)
estar (45)
estarcir (95)
estatalizar (26)

Verb Index

fallar (1)
fallecer (25)
fallir (47)
falsificar (80)
faltar (1)
familiarizar (26)
fanatizar (26)
farfullar (1)
fascinar (1)
fastidiar (1)
fatigar (61)
favorecer (25)
fecundar (1)
fecundizar (26)
federalizar (26)
felicitar (1)
fenecer (25)
fermentar (1)
fertilizar (26)
fervorizar (26)
festejar (1)
fiar (41)
fichar (1)
figurar (1)
fijar (1)
filmar (1)
filtrar (1)
finalizar (26)
financiar (1)
fincar (80)
fingir (32)
firmar (1)
fiscalizar (26)
fisgar (61)
flanquear (1)
flechar (1)
flexibilizar (26)
flexionar (1)

flirtear (1)
florar (1)
florecer (25)
flotar (1)
fluctuar (6)
fluir (23)
focalizar (26)
fomentar (1)
forcejear (1)
forjar (1)
formalizar (26)
formar (1)
fornicar (80)
forrar (1)
fortalecer (25)
fortificar (80)
forzar (10)
fosilizarse (26)
fotocopiar (1)
fotografiar (41)
fracasar (1)
fraccionar (1)
fragmentar (1)
fraguar (16)
franquear (1)
fraternizar (26)
fregar (58)
freír (46)
frenar (1)
frezar (26)
frivolizar (26)
frotar (1)
fructificar (80)
fruncir (95)
frustrar (1)
fugarse (61)
fulgir (32)
fulminar (1)

fumar (1)
fumigar (61)
funcionar (1)
fundamentar (1)
fundar (1)
fundir (3)
fungir (32)
fustigar (61)
galantear (1)
galopar (1)
galvanizar (26)
ganar (1)
gandulear (1)
gañir (47)
garantir (4)
garantizar (26)
garuar (6)
gasificar (80)
gastar (1)
gatear (1)
gemir (62)
generalizar (26)
generar (1)
germanizar (26)
germinar (1)
gestionar (1)
gimotear (1)
girar (1)
globalizar (26)
gloriarse (1)
glorificar (80)
glosar (1)
gobernar (63)
golpear (1)
gorjear (1)
gotear (1)
gozar (26)
grabar (1)

graduar (6)
granizar (26)
granjear (1)
granular (1)
gratificar (80)
gravar (1)
gravitar (1)
graznar (1)
gritar (1)
gruir (23)
gruñir (47)
guadañar (1)
guardar (1)
guarecer (25)
guarnecer (25)
guasearse (1)
guerrear (1)
guiar (41)
guiñar (1)
guionizar (26)
guisar (1)
gustar (1)
haber (48)
habilitar (1)
habitar (1)
habituar (6)
hablar (1)
hacer (49)
hacinar (1)
halagar (61)
hallar (1)
hamacar (80)
haraganear (1)
harinear (1)
hartar (1)
hastiar (41)
hebraizar (39)
hechizar (26)

heder (40)
helar (63)
helenizar (26)
henchir (62)
hender (40)
hendir (33)
heñir (74)
heredar (1)
herir (83)
hermanar (1)
hermetizar (26)
herrar (63)
hervir (83)
hibridizar (26)
hidratar (1)
hidrolizar (26)
higienizar (26)
hilar (1)
hilvanar (1)
hincar (80)
hinchar (1)
hipar (1)
hipnotizar (26)
hipotecar (80)
hipotetizar (26)
hispanizar (26)
histerizarse (26)
hocicar (80)
hojear (1)
holgar (77)
hollar (24)
homogeneizar (26)
homologar (61)
honrar (1)
horadar (1)
horripilar (1)
horrorizar (26)

hospedar (1)
hospitalizar (26)
hostigar (61)
hostilizar (26)
hozar (26)
huir (23)
humanizar (26)
humear (1)
humedecer (25)
humidificar (80)
humillar (1)
hundir (3)
hurgar (61)
huronear (1)
hurtar (1)
husmear (1)
idealizar (26)
idear (1)
identificar (80)
idiotizar (26)
ignorar (1)
igualar (1)
ilegalizar (26)
ilegitimar (1)
ilegitimizar (26)
iluminar (1)
ilustrar (1)
imaginar (1)
imbecilizar (26)
imbricar (80)
imbuir (23)
imitar (1)
impartir (3)
impedir (62)
impeler (2)
imperar (1)
impermeabilizar (26)

implicar (80)
implorar (1)
imponer (66)
importar (1)
importunar (1)
imposibilitar (1)
imprecar (80)
impregnar (1)
impresionar (1)
imprimir (50)
improbar (24)
improvisar (1)
impugnar (1)
impulsar (1)
impurificar (80)
imputar (1)
inaugurar (1)
incapacitar (1)
incautarse (1)
incendiar (1)
incensar (63)
incentivar (1)
incidir (3)
incinerar (1)
incitar (1)
inclinar (1)
incluir (23)
incomodar (1)
incomunicar (80)
incorporar (1)
increpar (1)
incrustar (1)
incubar (1)
inculcar (80)
inculpar (1)
incumbir (3)
incumplir (3)
incurrir (3)

indagar (61)
indemnizar (26)
indentar (1)
independizar (26)
indicar (80)
indignar (1)
indisponer (66)
individualizar (26)
indizar (26)
indoctrinar (1)
inducir (22)
indultar (1)
industrializar (26)
inestabilizar (26)
infantilizar (26)
infectar (1)
inferir (83)
infestar (1)
inflamar (1)
inflar (1)
infligir (32)
influenciar (1)
influir (23)
informar (1)
informatizar (26)
infrautilizar (26)
infringir (32)
infundir (3)
ingeniar (1)
ingerir (83)
ingresar (1)
inhibir (3)
inicializar (26)
iniciar (1)
injerir (83)

injertar (1)
injuriar (1)
inmergir (32)
inmiscuirse (23)
inmolar (1)
inmortalizar (26)
inmovilizar (26)
inmunizar (26)
inmutar (1)
innovar (1)
inquietar (1)
inquirir (7)
inscribir (44)
insensibilizar (26)
insertar (1)
insinuar (6)
insistir (3)
insolarse (1)
insonorizar (26)
inspeccionar (1)
inspirar (1)
instalar (1)
instar (1)
instaurar (1)
instigar (61)
instilar (1)
institucionalizar (26)
instituir (23)
instruir (23)
instrumentalizar (26)
insubordinarse (1)
insultar (1)
integrar (1)

Verb Index

intelectualizar (26)
intensificar (80)
intentar (1)
interactuar (6)
intercalar (1)
interceder (2)
intercomunicar (80)
interdecir (28)
interesar (1)
interferir (83)
interiorizar (26)
internacionalizar (26)
internalizar (26)
internar (1)
interpelar (1)
interponer (66)
interpretar (1)
interrogar (61)
interrumpir (3)
intervenir (90)
intimar (1)
intitular (1)
intoxicar (80)
intranquilizar (26)
intrigar (61)
intrincar (80)
introducir (22)
intuir (23)
inundar (1)
inutilizar (26)
invadir (3)
inventar (1)
inventariar (41)
invernar (63)

invertir (83)
investigar (61)
investir (62)
invitar (1)
invocar (80)
inyectar (1)
ionizar (26)
ir (51)
ironizar (26)
irrespetar (1)
irrigar (61)
irritar (1)
irrogar (61)
irrumpir (3)
islamizar (26)
itemizar (26)
izar (26)
jabonar (1)
jactarse (1)
jadear (1)
jalar (1)
jalbegar (61)
jalonar (1)
jerarquizar (26)
jeringar (61)
joder (2)
jorobar (1)
jubilar (1)
judaizar (39)
jugar (52)
juguetear (1)
juntar (1)
juramentar (1)
jurar (1)
justificar (80)
juzgar (61)
labializar (26)
laborar (1)

labrar (1)
lacar (80)
lacerar (1)
lacrar (1)
lactar (1)
ladear (1)
ladrar (1)
lagrimear (1)
laicizar (26)
lamber (2)
lamentar (1)
lamer (2)
laminar (1)
lamiscar (80)
languidecer (25)
lanzar (26)
lapidar (1)
largar (61)
lascar (80)
lastimar (1)
lateralizar (26)
latinizar (26)
latir (3)
lavar (1)
lazar (26)
leer (53)
legalizar (26)
legar (61)
legislar (1)
legitimar (1)
lenificar (80)
lentificar (80)
lesionar (1)
levantar (1)
levar (1)
lexicalizar (26)
liar (41)
libar (1)

martirizar (26)
mascar (80)
masculinizar
(26)
mascullar (1)
masificar (80)
masticar (80)
masturbarse (1)
materializar (26)
matizar (26)
maullar (14)
maximizar (26)
mecanizar (26)
mecanografiar
(41)
mecer (89)
mechificar (80)
mediatizar (26)
medicar (80)
medir (62)
melar (63)
memorizar (26)
mendigar (61)
menguar (16)
mentalizar (26)
mentar (63)
mentir (83)
mercantilizar
(26)
mercar (80)
merecer (25)
merendar (63)
merengar (61)
mesmerizar (26)
mestizar (26)
metabolizar (26)
metalizar (26)
meteorizar (26)

meter (2)
mexicanizar (26)
migar (61)
militarizar (26)
mimetizar (26)
minar (1)
mineralizar (26)
mingar (61)
miniaturizar (26)
minimalizar (26)
minimizar (26)
minusvalorizar
(26)
minutar (1)
mistificar (80)
mitificar (80)
mitigar (61)
mixtificar (80)
modernizar (26)
modificar (80)
modular (1)
moldear (1)
moler (56)
molestar (1)
molificar (80)
monedar (1)
monetizar (26)
monitorizar (26)
monologar (61)
monopolizar
(26)
monoptongar
(61)
montar (1)
montear (1)
moralizar (26)
morder (56)
mordicar (80)

morigerar (1)
morir (55)
mortificar (80)
mosquear (1)
mostrar (24)
motivar (1)
motorizar (26)
mover (56)
movilizar (26)
mudar (1)
mugir (32)
mullir (47)
multar (1)
multiplicar (80)
municipalizar
(26)
muñir (47)
murmurar (1)
musicar (80)
musitar (1)
mutilar (1)
nacer (57)
nacionalizar (26)
nadar (1)
narcotizar (26)
narrar (1)
nasalizar (26)
naturalizar (26)
naufragar (61)
navegar (61)
nebulizar (26)
necesitar (1)
negar (58)
negativizar (26)
negociar (1)
neutralizar (26)
nevar (63)
neviscar (80)

Verb Index

nidificar (80)
niquelar (1)
nivelar (1)
nobilizar (26)
nombrar (1)
nominalizar (26)
normalizar (26)
notar (1)
noticiar (1)
notificar (80)
nublarse (1)
nuclearizar (26)
numerar (1)
nutrir (3)
obcecar (80)
obedecer (25)
objetar (1)
oblicuar (1)
obligar (61)
obrar (1)
obscurecer (25)
obseder (2)
observar (1)
obsesionar (1)
obstaculizar (26)
obstar (1)
obstinarse (1)
obstruir (23)
obtener (86)
obviar (1)
ocasionar (1)
occidentalizar (26)
ocluir (23)
ocultar (1)
ocupar (1)
ocurrir (3)
odiar (1)

ofender (2)
oficializar (26)
ofrecer (25)
ofrendar (1)
ofuscar (80)
oír (59)
ojear (1)
oler (60)
olfatear (1)
oliscar (80)
olvidar (1)
omitir (3)
ondear (1)
ondular (1)
opacar (80)
operar (1)
operativizar (26)
opinar (1)
oponer (66)
opositar (1)
oprimir (3)
optar (1)
optimar (1)
optimizar (26)
opugnar (1)
orar (1)
ordenar (1)
ordeñar (1)
orear (1)
organizar (26)
orientalizar (26)
orientar (1)
originar (1)
orillar (1)
orinar (1)
orlar (1)
ornamentar (1)
ornar (1)

orzar (26)
osar (1)
oscilar (1)
oscurecer (25)
osificarse (80)
ostentar (1)
otear (1)
otorgar (61)
ovillar (1)
oxidar (1)
pacer (25)
pacificar (80)
pactar (1)
padecer (25)
paganizar (26)
pagar (61)
paladear (1)
palatalizar (26)
paliar (1)
palidecer (25)
palmotear (1)
palpar (1)
palpitar (1)
panificar (80)
panoramizar (26)
parabolizar (26)
paralizar (26)
parar (1)
parear (1)
parecer (25)
parir (3)
parlamentar (1)
parlotear (1)
parodiar (1)
parpadear (1)
participar (1)
particularizar (26)

147

partir (3)
pasar (1)
pasear (1)
pasmar (1)
pastar (1)
pasterizar (26)
pasteurizar (26)
patalear (1)
patear (1)
patentar (1)
patentizar (26)
patinar (1)
patrocinar (1)
patronizar (26)
pauperizar (26)
pecar (80)
pechar (1)
pedalear (1)
pedir (62)
peer (53)
pegar (61)
peinar (1)
pelar (1)
pelear (1)
peligrar (1)
pellizcar (80)
pelotear (1)
penalizar (26)
penar (1)
pencar (80)
pender (2)
penetrar (1)
pensar (63)
percatarse (1)
percibir (3)
percollar (24)
percudir (3)
percutir (3)

perder (40)
perdonar (1)
perdurar (1)
perecer (25)
perennizar (26)
perfeccionar (1)
perforar (1)
perjudicar (80)
perjurar (1)
permanecer (25)
permeabilizar (26)
permitir (3)
permutar (1)
perorar (1)
perpetrar (1)
perpetuar (6)
perseguir (82)
perseverar (1)
persignarse (1)
persistir (3)
personalizar (26)
personarse (1)
personificar (80)
persuadir (3)
pertenecer (25)
perturbar (1)
pervertir (83)
pervivir (3)
pesar (1)
pescar (80)
pestañear (1)
petrificar (80)
piar (41)
picar (80)
picotear (1)
pilllar (1)
pinchar (1)

pingar (61)
pintar (1)
pintear (1)
pintiparar (1)
pinzar (26)
pisar (1)
piscar (80)
pisotear (1)
pitar (1)
pizcar (80)
placar (80)
placer (64)
plagar (61)
planchar (1)
planear (1)
plagiar (1)
planificar (80)
plañir (47)
plantar (1)
plantear (1)
plantificar (80)
plasmar (1)
plastificar (80)
platicar (80)
plegar (58)
pluralizar (26)
poblar (24)
podar (1)
poder (65)
podrir (68)
poetizar (26)
polarizar (26)
polemizar (26)
polinizar (26)
politizar (26)
ponderar (1)
poner (66)
pontificar (80)

Verb Index

proseguir (82)
prosificar (80)
prosperar (1)
prostituir (23)
protagonizar (26)
proteger (21)
protestar (1)
proveer (53)
provenir (90)
provocar (80)
proyectar (1)
psicoanalizar (26)
publicar (80)
pudrir (68)
pugnar (1)
pulimentar (1)
pulir (3)
pulsar (1)
pulular (1)
pulverizar (26)
pungir (32)
puntear (1)
puntualizar (26)
puntuar (6)
punzar (26)
purgar (61)
purificar (80)
quebrantar (1)
quebrar (63)
quedar (1)
quejarse (1)
quemar (1)
querellarse (1)
querer (69)
quimerizar (26)
quintuplicar (80)

quitar (1)
rabiar (1)
racionalizar (26)
racionar (1)
radiar (1)
radicalizar (26)
radicar (80)
radiodifundir (3)
radiografiar (41)
raer (70)
rajar (1)
ralentizar (26)
rallar (1)
ramificarse (80)
rapar (1)
raptar (1)
rarificar (80)
rasar (1)
rascar (80)
rasgar (61)
rasguear (1)
rasguñar (1)
raspar (1)
rastrear (1)
rastrillar (1)
rasurarse (1)
ratificar (80)
rayar (1)
razonar (1)
reabrir (5)
reaccionar (1)
reactivar (1)
readquirir (7)
reafirmar (1)
reagrupar (1)
realizar (26)
realzar (26)
reanimar (1)

reanudar (1)
reaparecer (25)
reargüir (12)
reasentar (63)
reasumir (3)
reavivar (1)
rebajar (1)
rebanar (1)
rebasar (1)
rebatir (3)
rebautizar (26)
rebelarse (1)
reblandecer (25)
rebosar (1)
rebotar (1)
rebozar (26)
rebullir (47)
rebuscar (80)
rebuznar (1)
recabar (1)
recaer (19)
recalcar (80)
recalentar (63)
recalificar (80)
recapacitar (1)
recargar (61)
recatarse (1)
recelar (1)
receptar (1)
recesar (1)
rechazar (26)
rechinar (1)
recibir (3)
reciclar (1)
reciprocar (80)
recitar (1)
reclamar (1)
reclinar (1)

relampaguear (1)
relanzar (26)
relatar (1)
relativizar (26)
releer (53)
relegar (61)
relevar (1)
reliar (41)
relinchar (1)
rellenar (1)
relucir (54)
relumbrar (1)
remachar (1)
remangar (61)
remar (1)
remarcar (80)
rematar (1)
remecer (89)
remedar (1)
remediar (1)
rememorar (1)
remendar (63)
remeter (2)
remirar (1)
remitir (3)
remojar (1)
remolcar (80)
remoler (56)
remolinar (1)
remontar (1)
remorder (56)
remover (56)
remozar (26)
remplazar (26)
remunerar (1)
renacer (57)
rendir (62)
renegar (58)

reñir (74)
renovar (24)
rentabilizar (26)
rentar (1)
renunciar (1)
reorganizar (26)
reorientar (1)
repagar (61)
repanchigarse (61)
repantigarse (61)
reparar (1)
repartir (3)
repasar (1)
repatriar (41)
repeler (2)
repensar (63)
repentizar (26)
repercutir (3)
repertoriar (1)
repescar (80)
repetir (62)
repicar (80)
replegar (58)
replicar (80)
repoblar (24)
reponer (66)
reportar (1)
reportear (1)
reposar (1)
repostar (1)
reprender (2)
representar (1)
reprimir (3)
reprivatizar (26)
reprobar (24)
reprochar (1)
reproducir (22)

repudiar (1)
repudrir (68)
repugnar (1)
repujar (1)
repulir (3)
reputar (1)
requebrar (63)
requerir (83)
resaber (79)
resaltar (1)
resarcir (95)
resbalar (1)
rescatar (1)
rescindir (3)
rescontrar (24)
resecar (80)
reseñar (1)
resentirse (83)
reservar (1)
resfriar (41)
resguardar (1)
residir (3)
resignar (1)
resistir (3)
resollar (24)
resolver (93)
resonar (24)
resoplar (1)
respaldar (1)
respetar (1)
respingar (61)
respirar (1)
resplandecer (25)
responder (2)
responsabilizar (26)
resquebrajar (1)

trascolar (24)
trascordarse (24)
trasegar (58)
trasferir (83)
trasgredir (4)
trasladar (1)
traslucir (54)
trasnochar (1)
trasoír (59)
traspasar (1)
trasplantar (1)
trasponer (66)
trastocar (92)
trastornar (1)
trastrocar (92)
trasvasar (1)
trasvolar (24)
tratar (1)
traumatizar (26)
travestir (62)
trazar (26)
trenzar (26)
trepar (1)
trepidar (1)
triangular (1)
tributar (1)
trillar (1)
trincar (80)
trinchar (1)
tripitir (3)
triplicar (80)
tripular (1)
triscar (80)
trisecar (80)
triturar (1)
triunfar (1)
trivializar (26)
trizar (26)

trocar (92)
trompicar (80)
tronar (24)
tronchar (1)
tronzar (26)
tropezar (38)
trotar (1)
trucar (80)
truncar (80)
tullir (47)
tumbar (1)
tundir (3)
tupir (3)
turbar (1)
turnarse (1)
tutear (1)
tutelar (1)
ubicar (80)
ufanarse (1)
ulcerar (1)
ultimar (1)
ultrajar (1)
ulular (1)
uncir (95)
ungir (32)
unificar (80)
uniformar (1)
uniformizar (26)
unir (3)
universalizar (26)
untar (1)
uperizar (26)
urbanizar (26)
urdir (3)
urgir (32)
usar (1)
usurear (1)

usurpar (1)
utilizar (26)
vacar (80)
vaciar (41)
vacilar (1)
vacunar (1)
vadear (1)
vagar (61)
valer (88)
validar (1)
vallar (1)
valorar (1)
valorizar (26)
valuar (6)
vampirizar (26)
vanagloriarse (1)
vaporizar (26)
varar (1)
varear (1)
variar (41)
vedar (1)
vehiculizar (26)
vejar (1)
velar (1)
velarizar (26)
vencer (89)
vendar (1)
vender (2)
venerar (1)
vengar (61)
venir (90)
ventear (1)
ventilar (1)
ventiscar (80)
ventosear (1)
ver (91)
veranear (1)
verbalizar (26)

Verb Index

verdear (1)
verdecer (25)
verificar (80)
versar (1)
versificar (80)
verter (40)
vestir (62)
vetar (1)
viabilizar (26)
viajar (1)
vibrar (1)
viciar (1)
victimizar (26)
vidriar (41)
vigilar (1)
vigorizar (26)
vilipendiar (1)
vincular (1)
vindicar (80)
violar (1)
violentar (1)
virar (1)

virilizar (26)
visibilizar (26)
visitar (1)
vislumbrar (1)
vistar (1)
visualizar (26)
vitalizar (26)
vitorear (1)
vitrificar (80)
vituperar (1)
vivificar (80)
vivir (3)
vocalizar (26)
vocear (1)
vociferar (1)
volar (24)
volatilizar (26)
volcar (92)
voltear (1)
volver (93)
vomitar (1)
votar (1)

vulcanizar (26)
vulgarizar (26)
vulnerar (1)
xerografiar (41)
yacer (94)
yantar (1)
yuxtaponer (66)
zafarse (1)
zaherir (83)
zambucar (80)
zambullir (47)
zampar (1)
zangolotear (1)
zanjar (1)
zapatear (1)
zarandear (1)
zarpar (1)
zigzaguear (1)
zozobrar (1)
zumbar (1)
zurcir (95)
zurrar (1)

Appendix: Formation of Tenses

Non-reflexive verbs ending in -ar

hablar (to speak)

INDICATIVE

PRESENT	PRESENT PERFECT
hablo	he hablado
hablas	has hablado
habla	ha hablado
hablamos	hemos hablado
habláis	habéis hablado
hablan	han hablado

IMPERFECT	PLUPERFECT
hablaba	había hablado
hablabas	habías hablado
hablaba	había hablado
hablábamos	habíamos hablado
hablabais	habíais hablado
hablaban	habían hablado

PRETERITE	PAST ANTERIOR
hablé	hube hablado
hablaste	hubiste hablado
habló	hubo hablado
hablamos	hubimos hablado
hablasteis	hubisteis hablado
hablaron	hubieron hablado

FUTURE	FUTURE PERFECT
hablaré	habré hablado
hablarás	habrás hablado
hablará	habrá hablado
hablaremos	habremos hablado
hablaréis	habréis hablado
hablarán	habrán hablado

CONDITIONAL
hablaría
hablarías
hablaría
hablaríamos
hablaríais
hablarían

CONDITIONAL PERFECT
habría hablado
habrías hablado
habría hablado
habríamos hablado
habríais hablado
habrían hablado

SUBJUNCTIVE

PRESENT
SUBJUNCTIVE
hable
hables
hable
hablemos
habléis
hablen

PRESENT PERFECT
SUBJUNCTIVE
haya hablado
hayas hablado
haya hablado
hayamos hablado
hayáis hablado
hayan hablado

IMPERFECT
SUBJUNCTIVE
hablara/hablase
hablaras/hablases
hablara/hablase
habláramos/hablásemos
hablarais/hablaseis
hablaran/hablasen

PLUPERFECT
SUBJUNCTIVE
hubiera/hubiese hablado
hubieras/hubieses hablado
hubiera/hubiese hablado
hubiéramos/hubiésemos
hablado
hubierais/hubieseis hablado
hubieran/hubiesen hablado

IMPERATIVE

AFFIRMATIVE
-
habla
hable
hablemos
hablad
hablen

NEGATIVE
-
no hables
no hable
no hablemos
no habéis
no hablen

161

Non-reflexive verbs ending in -er

beber (to drink)

INDICATIVE

PRESENT
bebo
bebes
bebe
bebemos
bebéis
beben

PRESENT PERFECT
he bebido
has bebido
ha bebido
hemos bebido
habéis bebido
han bebido

IMPERFECT
bebía
bebías
bebía
bebíamos
bebíais
bebían

PLUPERFECT
había bebido
habías bebido
había bebido
habíamos bebido
habíais bebido
habían bebido

PRETERITE
bebí
bebiste
bebió
bebimos
bebisteis
bebieron

PAST ANTERIOR
hube bebido
hubiste bebido
hubo bebido
hubimos bebido
hubisteis bebido
hubieron bebido

FUTURE
beberé
beberás
beberá
beberemos
beberéis
beberán

FUTURE PERFECT
habré bebido
habrás bebido
habrá bebido
habremos bebido
habréis bebido
habrán bebido

CONDITIONAL	CONDITIONAL PERFECT
bebería	habría bebido
beberías	habrías bebido
bebería	habría bebido
beberíamos	habríamos bebido
beberíais	habríais bebido
beberían	habrían bebido

SUBJUNCTIVE

PRESENT SUBJUNCTIVE	PRESENT PERFECT SUBJUNCTIVE
beba	haya bebido
bebas	hayas bebido
beba	haya bebido
bebamos	hayamos bebido
bebáis	hayáis bebido
beban	hayan bebido

IMPERFECT SUBJUNCTIVE	PLUPERFECT SUBJUNCTIVE
bebiera/bebiese	hubiera/hubiese bebido
bebieras/bebieses	hubieras/hubieses bebido
bebiera/bebiese	hubiera/hubiese bebido
bebiéramos/bebiésemos	hubiéramos/hubiésemos bebido
bebierais/bebieseis	hubierais/hubieseis bebido
bebieran/bebiesen	hubieran/hubiesen bebido

IMPERATIVE

AFFIRMATIVE	NEGATIVE
-	-
bebe	no bebas
beba	no beba
bebamos	no bebamos
bebed	no bebáis
beban	no beban

Non-reflexive verbs ending in -ir

partir (to leave)

INDICATIVE

PRESENT
parto
partes
parte
partimos
partís
parten

PRESENT PERFECT
he partido
has partido
ha partido
hemos partido
habéis partido
han partido

IMPERFECT
partía
partías
partía
partíamos
partíais
partían

PLUPERFECT
había partido
habías partido
había partido
habíamos partido
habíais partido
habían partido

PRETERITE
partí
partiste
partió
partimos
partisteis
partieron

PAST ANTERIOR
hube partido
hubiste partido
hubo partido
hubimos partido
hubisteis partido
hubieron partido

FUTURE
partiré
partirás
partirá
partiremos
partiréis
partirán

FUTURE PERFECT
habré partido
habrás partido
habrá partido
habremos partido
habréis partido
habrán partido

CONDITIONAL	CONDITIONAL PERFECT
partiría	habría partido
partirías	habrías partido
partiría	habría partido
partiríamos	habríamos partido
partiríais	habríais partido
partirían	habrían partido

SUBJUNCTIVE

PRESENT SUBJUNCTIVE	PRESENT PERFECT SUBJUNCTIVE
parta	haya partido
partas	hayas partido
parta	haya partido
partamos	hayamos partido
partáis	hayáis partido
partan	hayan partido

IMPERFECT SUBJUNCTIVE	PLUPERFECT SUBJUNCTIVE
partiera/partiese	hubiera/hubiese partido
partieras/partieses	hubieras/hubieses partido
partiera/partiese	hubiera/hubiese partido
partiéramos/partiésemos	hubiéramos/hubiésemos partido
partierais/partieseis	hubierais/hubieseis partido
partieran/partiesen	hubieran/hubiesen partido

IMPERATIVE

AFFIRMATIVE	NEGATIVE
-	-
parte	no partas
parta	no parta
partamos	no partamos
partid	no partáis
partan	no partan

165

Reflexive verbs

levantarse (to get up)

INDICATIVE

PRESENT	PRESENT PERFECT
me levanto	me he levantado
te levantas	te has levantado
se levanta	se ha levantado
nos levanta	nos hemos levantado
os levantáis	os habéis levantado
se levantan	se han levantado

IMPERFECT	PLUPERFECT
me levantaba	me había levantado
te levantabas	te habías levantado
se levantaba	se había levantado
nos levantábamos	nos habíamos levantado
os levantabais	os habíais levantado
se levantaban	se habían levantado

PRETERITE	PAST ANTERIOR
me levanté	me hube levantado
te levantaste	te hubiste levantado
se levantó	se hubo levantado
nos levantamos	nos hubimos levantado
os levantasteis	os hubisteis levantado
se levantaron	se hubieron levantado

FUTURE	FUTURE PERFECT
me levantaré	me habré levantado
te levantarás	te habrás levantado
se levantará	se habrá levantado
nos levantaremos	nos habremos levantado
os levantaréis	os habréis levantado
se levantarán	se habrán levantado

CONDITIONAL
me levantaría
te levantarías
se levantaría
nos levantaríamos
os levantaríais
se levantarían

CONDITIONAL PERFECT
me habría levantado
te habrías levantado
se habría levantado
nos habríamos levantado
os habríais levantado
se habrían levantado

SUBJUNCTIVE

PRESENT
SUBJUNCTIVE
me levante
te levantes
se levante
nos levantemos
os levantéis
se levanten

PRESENT PERFECT
SUBJUNCTIVE
me haya levantado
te hayas levantado
se haya levantado
nos hayamos levantado
os hayáis levantado
se hayan levantado

IMPERFECT
SUBJUNCTIVE
me levantara/levantase
te levantaras/levantases
se levantara/levantase
nos levantáramos/
levantásemos
os levantarais/levantaseis
se levantaran/levantasen

PLUPERFECT
SUBJUNCTIVE
me hubiera/hubiese levantado
te huabieras/hubieses levantado
se hubiera/hubiese levantado
nos hubiéramos/hubiésemos
levantado
os hubierais/hubieseis levantado
se hubieran/hubiesen levantado

IMPERATIVE

AFFIRMATIVE
-
levántate
levántese
levantémonos
levantaos
levántense

NEGATIVE
-
no te levantes
no se levante
no nos levantemos
no os levantéis
no se levanten

Appendix